# Big Book Of Interesting Facts for Curious Kids

### *1492*

*Fun Facts About Science, Animals, History, Earth and Anything Else You Can Think Of for Smart Minds*

Omar Pickles

Big Book Of Interesting Facts for Curious Kids

1492 Fun Facts About Science, Animals, History, Earth and Anything Else You Can Think Of for Smart Minds

[Omar Pickles]

1st edition 2023

@ 2023 Omar Pickles

All rights reserved, in particular the right of reproduction, distribution and translation. No part of this work may be reproduced in any form (by photocopy microfilm or any other process) or stored, processed, duplicated or distributed using electronic systems without the written permission of the publisher.

Printed in the USA

# CONTENTS

**INTRODUCTION** ............................................................. 5

**CHAPTER 1: KIDS NEED TO KNOW IN DAILY LIFE** ............ 7
  Smart Kids Need to Know ............................................. 8
  Things We Have At Home ............................................ 12
  Facts About Our Pets .................................................. 14

**CHAPTER 2: SCIENCE AND TECHNOLOGY** ..................... 17
  For Einstein Juniors .................................................... 18
  For Science Geeks ....................................................... 22
  Knowledge About Technology .................................... 26

**CHAPTER 3: OUR PLANET** ............................................. 30
  Everything on Earth .................................................... 31
  Secrets of The Ocean .................................................. 39
  Secrets About Plants ................................................... 41
  Wet Facts About Rain Forests .................................... 45

**CHAPTER 4: THE BEAUTIFUL CONTINENT** ..................... 49
  African Things ............................................................. 50
  Chilly Facts About Antarctica ..................................... 53
  Amazing Asia ............................................................... 56
  Impressive Famous Places .......................................... 59

**CHAPTER 5: ENCYCLOPEDIC KNOWLEDGE OF BIOLOGY** . 62
  Facts About Animals In The Sky ................................. 63
  Proof That Animals Are Weird .................................... 65
  Dark Facts About Nocturnal Animals ......................... 72

## CHAPTER 6: OUR DIET .................................................. 76
Foodies Need To Know ........................................... 77
The Knowledge of Eating ........................................ 80

## CHAPTER 7: IMPRESSIVE GEOGRAPHY ........................... 90
Rocks, Minerals, And Gems ..................................... 91
Cave Facts To Explore ............................................. 95
Explosive Knowledge About Volcanic Eruptions ........ 98

## CHAPTER 8: TIME AND SPACE ...................................... 100
Impressive Things of Time ..................................... 101
Facts About Space Flight ....................................... 109
High-Flyng Facts About Airplanes .......................... 112
Out-Of-This-World Facts About Aliens .................... 115

## CHAPTER 9: DISTANT MATTER ..................................... 119
Old Knowledge About Ancient Civilizations ........... 120
About Dinosaurs, Ya Dig? ...................................... 122

## CHAPTER 10: THE MYSTERIES OF THE BODY ................ 126
Brain-Busting Brain .............................................. 127
Fantastic Things About The Five Senses ............... 130

# INTRODUCTION

Hi, guys! Welcome to the captivating universe of "Big Book Of Interesting Facts for Curious Kids: 1492 Fun Facts About Science, Animals, History, Earth, and Anything Else You Can Think Of for Smart Minds." It is with immense pleasure and enthusiasm that I invite you to delve into the rich tapestry of knowledge that this book unfolds. Here, we embark on a grand expedition, a literary adventure crafted to kindle the fires of curiosity and ignite the spark of imagination.

The world around us is an inexhaustible source of wonders and curiosities, and this book is your personal guide to navigate its intricate landscapes. Our primary goal is to foster an insatiable thirst for knowledge, and we believe that learning should be an exciting voyage. Whether you are a young scholar, a history buff, a nature aficionado, or just someone who is endlessly inquisitive, you will find this book to be a treasure trove of information and inspiration.

Within these pages, we embark on an exhilarating journey through various domains of knowledge. Science, with its marvels and mysteries, is our steadfast companion as we dive into the cosmos and explore the wonders of the microcosm. The animal kingdom, with its myriad of creatures, unveils incredible tales of adaptation, survival, and evolution. History, our time machine, takes us on a voyage through the annals of humanity, offering stories of triumph and tribulation. And the Earth, our beautiful blue planet, with its geological wonders and natural splendors, is presented for your admiration.

We firmly believe that learning should be an adventure in itself, and this book is designed to transform knowledge into an exhilarating journey of discovery. Each of the 1492 facts we've meticulously curated is like a bright gem, waiting to be discovered. These facts have been handpicked to engage your intellect, stimulate your creativity, and, most importantly, to leave you in awe of the world's remarkable complexity.

So, dear reader, I invite you to prepare for an expansive voyage of exploration and enlightenment. "Big Book Of Interesting Facts for Curious Kids" is more than a book; it's an open invitation to uncover the hidden wonders that surround us. In its pages, you will encounter inspiration, fascination, and an appreciation for the astonishing world we inhabit. Let us together embark on this exhilarating journey of discovery, where your quest for knowledge will be quenched and your love for learning will be invigorated. This book is your gateway to the world's wonders and a testament to the boundless curiosity that resides within us all.

# Chapter 1: Kids need to know in daily life

## Smart Kids Need to Know

1. The fear of trees is called dendrophobia.

2. Japan manufactured the first real toy robot, the Lilliput, which was a 15cm tall wind-up walking toy made from tinplate.

3. Today's numerical digits, such as 1, 2 and 3, are based on the Hindu-Arab numeral system created over 1000 years ago.

4. Television broadcasts use specific frequencies for broadcast, much like radio.

5. Recycling a glass jar will save enough energy for 3 hours of TV.

6. The use of search engines such as Google and Bing are one of the best and most regular ways to find information on the web. Google is currently the most popular search engine and receives hundreds of millions of search queries daily.

7. While bacteria can be treated with antibiotics, it is not effective against a virus.

8. The internets' domain name system includes top-level domains like .com, .info, .net, .org, .edu, .mil and .gov as well as country-specific domains and more.

9. The United States first introduced credit cards in the 1920's.

10. The fear of wide open areas is called agoraphobia.

11. The ranking of waste or 3 R's are reduce, reuse and recycle (in order of importance).

12. Potatoes used to be utilized as money on the island of Tristan da Cunha in the South Atlantic.

13. Four is the only number with the same number of letters.

14. The fear of reptiles is called Herpetophobia.

15. Nokia, Samsung, Motorola, Sony Ericsson, and Apple are examples of large mobile phone manufacturers.
The National Archives holds the original Declaration of Independence, the U.S. Constitution, and the Bill of Rights.

16. The British pound originally had the same value as a pound of silver.

17. Games such as Nintendogs, Brain Training, and Wii Sports by industry leader and pioneer Nintendo, have helped the video games industry grow and appeal to hardcore and casual gamers alike.

18. Leonardo da Vinci outlined designs for a humanoid robot in 1495. A lot of robot prototypes are being made today.

19. Many bygone presidents are shown on US dollar bills, such as George Washington ($1), Abraham Lincoln ($5), Andrew Jackson ($20), and Benjamin Franklin ($100).

20. Calvin Coolidge had a number of pets worthy of a zoo at the White House. He not only had a lot of dog breeds like terriers, a sheepdog, collies, and chows, but he also had cats, raccoons, a donkey, a bobcat, chickens, a wolf, an antelope, a wallaby, a pygmy hippo, and a few lion cubs.

21. You can hold more cold water with a sponge than hot water.

22. In English, the longest one-syllable phrase is ‹screeched›.

23. Over than 480 million people have played Monopoly.

24. The euro, Japanese yen and British pound are also heavily traded currencies.

25. The eggs' shell accounts for 12% of its weight.
You will find many different types of programs broadcast on television, such as news, sports, documentaries, sitcoms, reality TV, drama, movies, and commercials.

26. Room temperature ranges from 20 to 25C (68 to 77F).

27. For his theoretical physics research, Albert Einstein was awarded the Nobel Prize in Physics in 1921.

28. In addition to playing video games, television sets are also used to watch DVDs and Blu-ray disks through the use of a console.

29. The fear of trains is siderodromophobia.

30. A magnifying glass makes an image easier to see by using a convex lens' properties to enlarge it.

31. Glass balls are able to bounce higher than those made from rubber.

32. Anatidaephobia is the fear of being watched by a duck.

33. The fear of needles and sharp things is called aichmophobia

34. The number 2 is the only number larger than zero that gives you the same result when added or multiplied by itself (4).

35. History's shortest war carried on for just 38 minutes.

36. The euro is an example of a currency shared by countries in the European Union such as France, Germany, and Spain.

37. A tsunami can move at the same speed as a jet plane.

38. Money's buying power is, over time, lessened by inflation.

39. Advertising and subscriptions are ways that broadcasting companies use to earn money to pay for production costs.

40. Items such as animals and food were used as currency many thousands of years ago.

41. Employees will probably take leave more on a Monday than any other day of the week.

42. In 1878, the White House›s original phone number was simply the number 1. Before 1929, there was no telephone on the desk of the President in the Oval Office.

43. Woodrow Wilson, who is buried at the Washington National Cathedral, is the only president buried in DC.

44. Physical coins were first minted about 2500 years ago.

45. Neil Armstrong lands on the moon, with the use of the latest computing, robotics and space technology from the US.

46. In Sesame Street, the characters Bert and Ernie were modeled after Bert the policeman and Ernie the taxi driver from Frank Capra›s It›s a Wonderful Life.

47. Around 1970, plastic bottles were first implemented for soft drinks.

48. The common cold can be caused by more than 100 various types of viruses.

49. The first televisions were sold in the late 1920s.

## Things We Have At Home

50. Wrigley's gum became the first product to have a barcode.

51. A television works by receiving and showing signals of moving images.

52. Even though the technology was already available, color television sets were not common until the 1970s.

53. The acronym VHS is short for Video Home System.

54. There are fuses in all electrical appliances. Fundamentally, fuses are fire-breakers. If a power surge occurs, the fuse breaks down to prevent damage or explosion.

55. The bacteria in your ear can multiply 700 times if you wear headphones for just one hour. Creating a successful and high quality video game requires not only a lot of game developers, but also many graphic designers, programmers, managers, writers and musicians.

56. Japan invented Venetian blinds.

57. Today's screens are thin and use liquid crystal display (LCD) and plasma, which have replaced the earlier cathode ray tubes (CRT).

58. Wine sours when exposed to light, which is why they are sold in tinted bottles.

59. Computers are not only the machines that sit on our desks, but they are also built into smaller things like phones, toys, appliances and music players. Sometimes we do not even realize we are using a computer.

60. 1908 saw the invention of the teabag.

61. Before toothpaste, the Colgate company manufactured starch, soap, and candles.

62. The first cellphones were very bulky, but they are now thin, small, and portable with rechargeable batteries, and have become invaluable tools for people all over the world to keep in contact.

63. The dirtiest thing in a normal household, hospital, or hotel room is the TV remote.

64. The dishwasher was designed in the year 1889.

65. Since 1935, the dollar values on the Monopoly board game have not changed.

66. Refrigeration extends the life of rubber bands.

67. The first doorbell was created in 1831.

68. To make an average tie takes 110 silkworm cocoons.

69. Remote controls were introduced in the 1980s.

70. In his car factory, Henry Ford creates the world's first moving conveyor belt-based assembly line, which can put together a Model T in 93 minutes.

71. Monopoly was originally designed as a circle.

72. In 1900, the first vacuum-packed ground coffee was introduced.

73. A television also emits sound through speakers.

74. Fish scales are an ingredient in certain lipsticks.

75. Household dust is composed of dead skin cells.

76. Created around the 1940s, electronic computers were as big as a large room.

77. The pictures on a TV screen refresh so fast that the human eye perceives them as smooth motion.

78. The World Wide Web is all the pages and sites that are accessible on the internet through a web browser. Although the two are not the same thing, it is often referred to as the internet, which is actually the large collection of networks that connects computers from around the globe.

79. The first Robotics Inventions System is revealed by LEGO.

## *Facts About Our Pets*

80. Goldfish are capable of seeing both infrared and ultraviolet light.

81. An ostrich can run faster than a horse and the male ostrich rumbles like a lion.

82. African Grey Parrots can say than 200 words.

83. The ear of a cat has 32 muscles.

84. Pigs are unable to look up at the sky.

85. Cats have no collar bones, and they have very supple spines. When a cat walks, its back paws move in almost the same spot where its front paws were before, which makes less noise and leave less traces on the ground.

86. In order to feed their babies, both male and female pigeons make something called crop milk. Very few birds are able to do it; doves, greater flamingos, and emperor penguins do.

87. There are more than 340 dog breeds, that all come from the same type of wild wolf that existed many years ago.

88. The cat door was created by Isaac Newton.

89. Horses stand up when they sleep.

90. Huskies can run as fast as approximately 31 km per hour, but stamina is their best ability.

91. Cats can leap up to seven times the length of their tail.

92. The Chihuahua is the smallest dog.

93. A hen lays an average of 228 eggs annually.

94. There are millions of tiny hairs in a gecko's foot that can adhere to surfaces with a special chemical bond and allows it to climb walls and hold on using just one toe.

95. Black-light makes cat urine glow.

96. Dogs have two separate air passages, one breathing passage and one smelling passage. It helps them to retain scents even while breathing out through the nose.

97. Typically, small dogs will outlive larger breeds.

98. The greyhound is the fastest dog, capable of achieving speeds of up to 45 mph (72kph).

99. About 10% of all the bones of a cat are in its tail.

100. Cats have a 285-degree peripheral vision.

101. The nose of a dog is like a human fingerprint – special to its owner.

102. The tail of a cat holds almost 10% of all the bones in its body.

103. A cat uses its whiskers to judge if there is too little room to fit through.

# Chapter 2: Science and Technology

## For Einstein Juniors

104. The paper On Computable Numbers, which begins the computer revolution, is released by Alan Turing.

105. In the 1970s, coin-operated video games were introduced, and popular titles included Computer Space and Pong.

106. Tropical storms and hurricanes were officially given names from 1953.

107. The original AIBO, a robotic dog that can learn, do tricks and communicate, is launched by Sony. Upgrades have since been created.

108. The White House was only completed a year after George Washington died so he never lived in DC. The first to live there was his successor, John Adams.

109. There are 158 verses in the Greek national anthem.

110. 1 megabyte equals 1 048 576 bytes.

111. The fear of bathing is Ablutophobia.

112. A computer uses many peripheral input/output devices like a keyboard, mouse, screen, hard drive, and a printer to exchange information.

113. The highest wind turbine's rotor tips measure more than 656 feet above the ground.

114. Until they are fifty years old, oak trees do not bear acorns.

115. The government owns 32 percent of all U.S. property.

116. Digital transmissions have replaced the old analog system. Just like the information on a computer, digital transmissions use 0' and 1s, which are more reliable than traditional analog broadcasts.

117. It took 20 years for Charles Darwin, an English naturalist, to write and publish his original book On the Origin of Species detailing the evolution process.

118. Fossils are proof of species that have died out. Perfect circumstances are required for the formation of fossils though.

119. A gigayear is 1,000,000,000,000 years.

120. Computers can be linked to create networks which allow users to share data from different locations. Examples of such networks are local area networks (LAN) and wide area networks (WAN) which connect areas of various sizes. The Internet is a large network of global computers that allows users to access their email and other applications.

121. You could fit almost 900 trillion footballs into the Grand Canyon.

122. Another main part of natural selection is instinct, which is for example, how birds know to migrate to warmer climates in winter in order to survive.

123. The first programmable robot arm, which later became the first industrial robot used to complete risky and repetitive tasks on the assembly line at General Motors in 1962, was designed by George Devol and Joe Engelberger.

124. With electrical shocks of around 500 volts, electric eels can daze both their predators and their prey.

125. There are 420 chairs on a normal 747 jumbo jet.

126. The first keys and ignitions for cars were implemented in 1949.

127. Andrew Jackson›s statue in Lafayette Square (directly across from the White House) was partly made of British cannons used in the 1812 war. It was the first statue of a horse created in the United States as well.

128. On May 25, 1910, the Wright Brothers took a six-minute flight piloted by Orville and with Wilbur being the passenger. This is the only time they ever flew together.

129. The first Star Wars film by George Lucas is released, motivating a new generation of researchers with his vision of a shared future with robots like the now famous R2-D2 and C-3PO.

130. In 1911, the first U.S. coast-to-coast airplane flight lasted 49 days.

131. Before DVDs and Blu-ray disks, we used video cassettes, but these have been replaced by new technology since the late 1990s.

132. Pi cannot be conveyed as a fraction, which makes it an irrational number. When written as a decimal, it does not repeat and does not end.

133. Rio de Janeiro means River of January.

134. Japan, Jordan, and San Marino's national anthems each have only 4 lines.

135. Computers work by carrying out simple commands like adding up numbers and moving data around.

136. The area of multiplayer games has expanded through internet gaming, which has allowed players to interact with others in different cities and even different countries.

137. Many large automatons were already designed between the 1700s to 1900s, such as the mechanical duck created by Jacques de Vaucanson, that could crane its neck, flap its wings and swallow food.

138. During their lives, the average American can eat more than 465 trees worth of paper.

139. The smallest robot, a helicopter measuring 7cm high and weighing 10 grams, is released by Epsom. It is intended to be a flying camera during natural disasters.

140. There is carbon in every living thing on Earth.

141. In the summer, when Abraham Lincoln stayed at the Soldiers' Home, he used to ride his horse the four miles to the White House and back.

142. It takes more than 50,000 years for a plastic container to begin decomposing.

143. 1 Googol is the number 1 with 100 zeros.

144. The Library of Congress, with its collection of over 162 million items, is the world's biggest library. With around 12 000 items added daily to the collections, this number is constantly growing.

145. Red light's wavelength is the largest.

146. Disney Studios released the first full-length animated film in 1937, which was Snow White and the seven dwarfs.

147. Sir Tim Berners-Lee, an English physicist, is known to have invented the World Wide Web in 1989. He has since continued to create web standards and other projects related to the internet.

148. Worries over safety and privacy have always been a problem on the Internet, with many users still unaware of the possible risks they take when accessing confidential data, passwords and personal information on different websites. Viruses and spam emails are other causes of security concerns that often cause web users delays and headaches.

149. The burning of fossil fuels consumes more than 86% of the energy used in the United States.

150. As a technique of identification, the Chinese used fingerprints as far back as AD 700.

151. In his play called Rossums Universal Robots, Karel Capek uses the word 'robot' to describe devices that imitate humans. It was about a world where the robots enslaved the humans they once served.

152. The first computers created around the 1940s differ a lot from today's versions. Unlike our modern portable laptops, they took up an entire room and used a lot of power.

## *For Science Geeks*

153. When it freezes, water swells by 9%. Ice weighs less than water, which is why it floats.

154. The body emits a tiny amount of light so weak the eye cannot see it.

155. Petrol has no common freezing point (it can freeze anywhere from -82 to -115C (-180 and -240F).

156. Through combining charcoal, saltpeter and sulphur, gunpowder is made.

157. The Turing Test, to establish if a machine is capable of self-thought, is proposed by Alan Turing. It tests if, during a conversation, a machine is indistinguishable from a human.

158. As the skates and boards used by snowboarders and ice skaters heat up the snow around them, they glide on thin ice!

159. Depending on how complex the computer program is, it can have anything from a few to a few million commands, and present-day applications like image editors and word processors can require a lot of time and a lot of people to complete it.

160. Wind power works by using windmills, sails etc. to use energy from the wind. As emission is low, it is a clean source of power.

161. Iron›s atomic symbol is Fe (Ferric was the original name for iron).

162. Mathematical and scientific knowledge is the way in which engineers solve practical problems. The word Engineer is derived from Latin, meaning "cleverness."

163. Ancient Egyptians used concepts of geometry as far back as 3000 BC, using, among other formulas, equations to estimate the field of circles.

164. Clouds appear white as they reflect sunlight from above.

165. Natural gas is odorless, it has strong smells added to it so that we can detect leaks.

166. Pythagoras was a Greek philosopher and mathematician, who created the Pythagorean theorem of $a^2 + b^2 = c^2$, around 500 BC. It related to the three sides of the right-angle triangle.

167. The speed of sound travels at approximately 1,230 km/h (767 mph).

168. The symbols used to add (+) and subtract (-) have been around for thousands of years, but most mathematical symbols were only created in the 16th century. Math calculations were written in words before this time, which made it very time-consuming.

169. Scientists think that people who dream of an activity will actually improve it in real life.

170. The compass and straight edge were important geometry development devices, allowing different lengths, angles, and geometric shapes to be created.

171. Archimedes of Syracuse lived about 250 BC and played a major role in the development of geometry including a method for measuring the volume of irregular shaped objects.

172. A computer has two types of memory, read-only memory or ROM, and random access memory or RAM. The memory stores information that can be accessed by the computer›s CPU to perform actions. Software data and information that can only be read is stored in ROM, while the computer can access and write to RAM at any time.

173. While the value of pi is today calculated to 1.2411 trillion decimal places, back in the 17th century it was only done to 35.

174. The numbers of the Fibonacci sequence are 0, 1, 1, 2, 3, 5, 8, 13, 21, 34, 55, 89, 144, 233, 377, 610, 987,......

175. Born in 1882, Emmy Noether was identified by Einstein as the most influential woman in mathematics history. She was a German mathematician who contributed significantly to abstract algebra and theoretical physics.

176. Asimov's Three Laws of Robotics are: 1. A robot may not injure a human being or, through inaction, allow a human being to come to harm. 2. A robot must obey any orders given to it by human beings, except where such orders would conflict with the First Law.3. A robot must protect its own existence as long as such protection does not conflict with the First or Second Law.

177. A bolt of lightning will reach 30 000 degrees Celsius (54 000 degrees Fahrenheit). This is about six times as hot as the sun's surface. While a lightning bolt may look big, it›s actually only as long as a ballpoint pen.

178. Just to withstand wind resistance when moving at a speed of 80 km/h (50 mph), cars consume about half of their fuel. Water consists of 2 parts hydrogen and one part oxygen ($H_2O$).

179. Food energy is typically measured in calories or joules.

180. Modern geometry has developed in a number of areas, including those making use of today's computers' raw computing power.

181. Most tennis rackets have a string tension of between 50 and 70 pounds. Low tension gives less control and more power, and high tension gives more control and less power.

182. The research of thunder is called brontology.

183. Lightning can strike twice.
Humidity (not air) causes drying of super glue.

184. Sound moves fifteen times quicker through steel than air.

185. Isaac Newton invented the physics laws and put together many influential infinitesimal calculus ideas.

186. Light journeys from the sun to Earth in 8 minutes and 19 seconds.

187. Water can operate against gravity, in a process called capillary motion, moving up narrow tubes.

188. Touching poison ivy results in an allergic reaction on the skin because it creates a skin irritant called urushiol.

## Knowledge About Technology

189. Email has been around longer than the World Wide Web.

190. To send an email in the 1980s, you had to use a computer and a rotary telephone to connect to a service called Micronet.

191. There were no URLs in those days. Instead, Web pages had numbers.

192. Microsoft, Apple, Google, and HP were all started in garages.

193. Computer programming is one of the fastest-growing occupations.

194. Windows' original name was Interface Manager.

195. The Apple II had a hard drive of just 5 megabytes when it was released in 1977.

196. Technophobia is the fear of technology.

197. Cyberphobia is the fear of computers.

198. Nomophobia is the fear of being without a cell phone.

199. About 51 percent of Internet traffic is non-human.

200. Most of that traffic is made up of hacking, spamming, and phishing.

201. The average computer user blinks 7 times a minute. The normal rate is 20 times a minute.

202. The first computer was almost 8 feet (2.5 meters) tall and weighed more than 66,000 pounds (30,000 kg).

203. About 8 billion devices are connected to the Internet.

204. More than 570 new websites are created every minute.

205. More video content is uploaded to YouTube in a 60-day period than the three major US television networks created in 60 years.

206. An estimated 340,000 tweets are sent per minute.

207. About 500 million tweets are sent per day.

208. Over 4.2 billion data records were stolen in 2016.

209. Approximately 250 million hours of TV shows and movies are watched daily via Netflix.

210. More than 56 million hours of music is streamed daily.

211. The amount of technical information doubles every two years.

212. Domain name registrations were free until 1995.

213. More than 2.3 billion people own an iPhone.

214. In 2013, Amazon had 1,000 robots operating in its warehouses. Now Amazon has 45,000 robots operating across 20 warehouses.

215. About 47 percent of jobs will disappear in the next 25 years as robots replace human workers.

216. Roughly 92 percent of the world's currency is digital.

217. Most large banking transactions are done digitally and not with cash.

218. IBM launched RAMAC in 1956.

219. RAMAC stood for Random Access Method of Accounting and Control.

220. RAMAC was the first computer to save data on randomly accessible hard drives.

221. On RAMAC, 5 megabytes of data weighed a ton.

222. The first computer mouse was invented by Douglas Engelbart in 1968.

223. The first mouse was made of wood.

224. Engelbart called the device a "mouse" because the cable at the end of the device looked like a mouse's tail.

225. Wikipedia uses anti-vandal bots to make sure people don't edit articles with false information.

226. The word robot comes from the Czech word robota, which means "work."

227. Credit card chip technology has been around since 1986.

228. November 30 is Computer Security Day.

**28**

229. The barcode was invented in 1952. But it wasn't used to label products until 1974.

230. Nintendo was founded in 1889. Back in those days, the company made playing cards.

231. Amazon started as an online bookstore called Cadabra.com.

232. The first cell phone call was made in New York City in 1973.

233. The first text message was sent in 1992.

234. The text message read, "Merry Christmas."

235. More people have cell phones than have indoor toilets.

236. The first Web page has been running since 1991.

237. The top three most-used passwords are 123456, password, and 12345.

238. About 220 million tons of old computers and other devices are thrown away in the United States every year.

# Chapter 3: Our Planet

# *Everything on Earth*

239. 71% of the earth's surface is made up of the ocean.

240. Earth is not a perfect sphere. It is actually closer to the shape of an egg.

241. Only 7% of the ocean is covered with sea ice.

242. Libya is the hottest place on Earth. The highest temperature that was ever recorded there was 136 degrees Fahrenheit in the year 1922.

243. Earth is not a perfect sphere because the strength of gravity around it is uneven.

244. The Great Barrier Reef is so large it can be seen from the moon.

245. Antarctica is the coldest place on Earth.

246. There are only three countries in the world that have not adopted the metric system.

247. Coral reefs are the largest living structures in the world. They are the only natural home that is also living.

248. In the summer, due to the metal expanding in the heat, the Eiffel Tower can grow up to six inches taller.

249. Columbus originally believed that the earth was actually shaped like a pear.

250. A blue moon, in which the moon appears blue and full, only appears once in 2.7 years.

251. The earth is struck by lightning at least 6,000 times per minute!

252. The biggest island in the world is Greenland.

253. China is one of the most elongated (meaning greater in length) countries in the world.

254. There are around 45,000 thunderstorms occurring around the world every day.

255. For some reason, the average Canadian earns more than the average American and is therefore richer.

256. There are around 1,500 earthquakes in Japan happening every year.

257. Diamonds actually are not as rare as you may think. They are very easy to find on Earth.

258. Lightning strikes the earth 100 times a second!

259. It is not illegal to escape from prison in Denmark.

260. The Kawah Ijen volcano in Indonesia has luminous blue lava and a massive acid lake.

261. Only about 10% of the earth's population lives in the southern hemisphere.

262. On average, the ocean is about 2.7 miles deep.

263. Hurricanes that appear over the ocean can last up to ten days.

264. Around 8.5 million tons of water evaporates from the Dead Sea every day.

265. 85% of all Earth's plant life is found in the ocean.

266. The only continent on Earth that does not have an active volcano is the continent Australia.

267. The water in the Atlantic Ocean is saltier than the water in the Pacific Ocean.

268. Hawaii and New York are the two states surrounded by the most ocean water.

269. Spanish, Mandarin Chinese, and English are the three most common languages spoken in the whole world.

270. Perth is the windiest city in Australia.

271. People in Switzerland eat the most chocolate: 22 pounds per person a year.

272. Yonge Street in Toronto, Canada, is the longest street in the whole world. It is 1,178 miles long.

273. The original name for Australia was "New Holland."

274. The Grand Canyon is so large it can hold up to 900 trillion footballs.

275. The smallest ocean in the world is the Arctic Ocean.

276. Half of the world's oxygen supply is produced by the Amazon rainforest.

277. The country Brazil was named after a tree.

278. The country Brazil makes up 50% of the South American continent.

279. There are around 120 different rivers in Jamaica.

280. The Great Wall of China is around 3,995 miles long.

281. Approximately 50% of the world's population uses rice as a staple food.

282. India has over 200 million cows and 100,000 post offices, the most in the world for both.

283. There are more redheads in Scotland than in any other country in the world.

284. The world's largest collection of flora can be found in Bali.

285. The original name for Hawaii was the "Sandwich Islands."

286. The country of Germany is the border for nine other countries.

287. There are more pyramids in Peru than there are in Egypt.

288. Tokyo was once called "Edo."

289. The world's oceans contain 200 times more gold than has already been mined.

290. Around 75% of the world's countries are north of the equator.

291. The original name for New York was "New Amsterdam."

292. The Dead Sea is not part of the sea. It is actually a lake located inland.

293. Saudi Arabia has absolutely no rivers.

294. The water in the Dead Sea is so salty that it is easy to float on the water and almost impossible to sink.

295. Cuba is the largest exporter of sugar in the world.

296. Hawaii only became part of the United States in the 1900s.

297. There are 571 miles of shoreline in New York.

298. Rio de Janeiro can be translated into the "River of January."

299. Up to 32% of land in the United States is owned by the U.S. government.

300. New Zealand's South Island is the oldest exposed surface on Earth.

301. The typical height of a tsunami wave in the Pacific Ocean is between 19.7 feet to 29.5 feet high.

302. The Earth weighs 6,588,000,000,000,000,000 tons. What a mouthful!

303. Up to 80% of the world's food crops are pollinated by insects.

304. The deepest living fish discovered in the oceans is known as the "ghost fish," and it lives 26,715 feet deep.

305. The largest known blue whale to live is known to be the same height as an 11-story building.

306. About 97% of the world's habitable space is in the oceans.

307. Sicily is the largest island in the Mediterranean Sea.

308. Canada has more lakes than any other country in the entire world.

309. Up to 90% of the world's volcanic activity occurs in the ocean.

310. The Nile River in Egypt is known to always flow north.

311. The earth will experience over 50,000 earthquakes, on average, in an entire year.

312. The average iceberg will weigh around 20,000,000 tons.

313. About 98% of Antarctica is ice while the other 2% is barren rock.

314. Every single living thing on Earth contains a certain amount of carbon.

315. A mature oak tree will shed around 700,000 leaves during autumn.

316. The continent of Asia covers around 30% of the land on Earth but holds 60% of the world's population.

317. Earth's atmosphere is around 60 miles thick.

318. The Dead Sea is the lowest point that can be found on land. It is 1,388 feet below sea level.

319. Scientists suggest that life on Earth used to be purple rather than green.

320. Every day dust from space falls to Earth, and its particles are so small that we cannot see them.

321. The General Sherman giant sequoia is a tree, and it is the biggest living thing on Earth.

322. The Great Barrier Reef is the world's largest living structure.

323. Earth formed at the same time as the rest of the solar system, so all of the planets are around the same age as Earth.

324. Earth is the third rock from the sun and it is the fifth-largest rock in the solar system.

325. The ocean is one of the most used means of transport across the globe, mostly by shipping companies and not actual people.

326. The Pacific Ocean's name can be translated into "peaceful sea."

327. The Arctic Ocean is completely covered in sea ice during the winter.

328. The third-largest ocean is the Indian Ocean, and it only takes up about 14% of the earth's surface.

329. The Bermuda Triangle, one of the biggest mysteries on Earth, is located in the Atlantic Ocean.

330. You will find turtles living on every single continent in the world except Antarctica.

331. Earthquakes actually move the earth underneath the ocean, and that is what causes large waves that turn into tsunamis.

332. You will find spiders everywhere on Earth except in Antarctica.

333. It is suspected that up to 2,000 new species are discovered either in our oceans or on the land every year.

334. The Sargasso Sea is the only sea that does not have a coastline.

335. Earth's core is as hot as the sun's surface.

336. The Yew Tree is the most toxic plant on Earth.

337. Only 0.0003% of the water on Earth can safely be used by humans.

338. Earth is electric and slightly radioactive.

339. Hudson Bay, in Canada, has the lowest gravity of any part of the earth.

340. Dolphins in the ocean are typically blue, but the dolphins in the Amazon River are usually pink.

341. There is a type of mushroom that grows on Earth that if you eat it once, you will feel fed for the rest of your life.

342. The distance from New York to Los Angeles is greater than the diameter of the moon!

343. Eight out of ten of the most expensive disasters in the history of the United States have been due to hurricanes.

344. An Australian man attempted to sell New Zealand on eBay in 2006.

345. A type of rainbow can be created from the light of the moon, and it is called a moonbow.

346. A place on Earth called "Ethiopia" has a 13-month long year, and they are still living in the year 2009.

347. The Opah is the only warm-blooded fish species in the whole world.

348. Scuba diving in the ocean is safer than skydiving, driving, and even running a marathon.

349. One inch of the ocean's depth contains as much water as Earth's atmosphere.

350. There is 50 times more carbon in the ocean than there is in the earth's atmosphere.

351. Only eight feet of the ocean's depth can hold as much heat as the earth's atmosphere.

352. If all the mid-ocean ridges were combined, they could stretch around the earth twice.

353. 702 feet is the deepest free dive into the ocean that anyone has ever done.

354. 1,090 feet and 4.5 inches are the deepest anyone has ever scuba dived into the ocean.

355. The deepest dive into the ocean mankind has ever done, using a manned vessel, was 36,089 feet.

356. The largest earthquake ever recorded was in Alaska in 2016.

357. Some people believe that you can see The Great Wall of China from space, but you actually cannot.

358. Humans, and most other things on Earth, are made up of the same material that stars are made out of.

## *Secrets of The Ocean*

359. The only fish that is known to blink with both eyes is the shark.

360. A long time ago, whales used to walk on land!

361. Sea Lions are the only known animal that can clap in rhythm.

362. In contrast to most fish, instead of scales, seahorses are coated in bony plates.

363. Just 18 of the 250 + recognized shark species are considered to be dangerous to humans.

364. The swordfish is the quickest fish in the sea and can achieve speeds of up to 108kph (68 mph).

365. Although both are aquatic, dolphins have evolved from mammals, while sharks have descended from ancestors of fish.

366. The eyes of a seahorse can move independently, to better search for food and predators in the water.

367. Through ramming them with their snout, dolphins will kill sharks.

368. When sleeping, one half of a dolphin's brain remains alert.

369. The largest living species is the blue whale that can reach up to 100 feet.

370. Lobster blood does not have a color, but it turns blue when exposed to air.

371. Many people think that dehydration and manatees can explain early mermaid sightings.

372. Killer Whales, or Orcas, are not really whales, but rather the biggest type of dolphins that exist.

373. For more than 400 million years, sharks have been around.

374. Jellyfish are not fish. They don't have a brain, heart, or bones.

375. Jellyfish have no brains.

376. The giant squid has the world's biggest eyes.

377. The embryos of tiger sharks already start fighting with each other in their mother's womb, before birth.

378. The Giant Pacific Octopus can fit its whole body through a hole as small as its beak.

379. A shrimp›s heart is situated in its head.

380. The sea otter has thicker fur than any other mammal. A grown male can have about 800 million hairs, while a human has only 5 million.

381. Dolphins can hear sounds underwater from 24 km (15 miles) away.

382. A collection of jellyfish is called a smack.

383. At 4 km (2.5miles) away, sharks can sense a drop of blood.

384. Dolphins have been observed covering their long snouts with sea sponge to shield them from getting hurt when searching for food.

385. A blue whale is as heavy as up to thirty elephants and long as three big tour buses.

386. Providing each piece still has part of the central disk, you can divide a starfish into five pieces, and each piece will live.

## *Secrets About Plants*

387. Dendrochronology is the science of calculating a tree's age by counting its rings.

388. Brazil is named after a tree.

389. Eighty-five percent of plant life is found in the ocean.

390. An average tree provides enough wood to make 170,100 pencils.

391. Without plants, there would be no life on Earth.

392. The first type of aspirin came from the bark of a willow tree.

393. The Amazon rain forest produces half the world's oxygen supply.

394. Washington, DC's famous cherry blossom trees were a gift to the United States from Tokyo, Japan, in 1912.

395. Bamboo is the fastest-growing woody plant in the world.

396. Bamboo can grow 3 feet (1 meter) in a single day.

397. The ginkgo is one of the oldest species of tree, dating back 250 million years.

398. There are more than 300,000 plant species.

399. During the 1600s, tulips were worth more than gold in Holland.

400. The African baobab tree can store thousands of gallons (liters) of water in its trunk.

401. Oak trees don't produce acorns until they are about 50 years old.

402. A sunflower looks like one giant flower, but it is actually made of hundreds of tiny flowers called florets.

403. Sunflowers are the symbol of nuclear disarmament.

404. A sunflower's roots can extract radioactive material through their roots and store them in their stems and leaves.

405. Trees are the longest-lived organisms on Earth.

406. In 2012, Russian scientists resurrected a 32,000-year-old extinct Arctic flowering plant using seeds found in Ice Age squirrel burrows.

407. A cactus can store large amounts of water in its trunk.

408. Cacti have very long roots that can soak up water deep underground.

409. A cactus is covered with a waxy substance to prevent water from evaporating from its surface.

410. Some species of cacti can live for hundreds of years.

411. Almost all species of cacti are native to the Americas.

412. Sundews, pitcher plants, and Venus flytraps all capture insects and eat them.

413. One type of orchid grows underground. It was discovered in Australia in 1928.

414. The largest flower in the world is the Rafflesia.

415. Rafflesia smells like rotting meat.

416. About 70,000 plant species are used for medicine.

417. About 80 percent of the Earth's original forests have been destroyed.

418. Roughly 90 percent of the foods we eat come from just 30 plants.

419. Oak trees are struck by lightning more than any other tree.

420. More than a million trees were planted in Nebraska in 1876 to celebrate the first Arbor Day.

421. The first apple seeds came to America from Europe in 1623.

422. Morning glory flowers open every morning and close every evening.

423. The leaves of poison ivy aren't its only dangerous part; smoke from burning this plant is also toxic.

424. The first plant to grow after the 1980 volcanic eruption of Mount Saint Helens in Washington was a purple prairie lupine.

425. A huge underground vault holds almost a billion seeds for safekeeping.

426. Mosses and ferns produce spores instead of seeds.

427. The gemstone amber is actually fossilized tree resin.

428. Balsa trees only bloom at night.

429. The stem of a sugar cane can grow to be more than 17 feet (5 meters) tall.

430. Corn is the most planted field crop in the United States.

431. Epiphytes are plants that grow on other plants for support.

432. Epiphytes have no roots.

433. Most epiphytes are found in tropical places.

434. Epiphytes do not harm the plants they grow on.

435. Parasitic plants do harm their hosts.

436. Parasitic plants take nutrients from their hosts and can actually kill the host plant.

# Wet Facts About Rain Forests

437. Rain forests cover about 6 percent of Earth's land.

438. The largest rain forests are in South America, Southeast Asia, and western Africa.

439. Tropical rain forests are located near the equator.

440. Tropical rain forests are very warm, with temperatures around 86°F (30°C).

441. Temperate rain forests are cooler than tropical rain forests.

442. They are located in the northwestern parts of North America, New Zealand, and a few other countries.

443. Rain forests are found on every continent except Antarctica.

444. Brazil and Indonesia have the largest amount of rain forest.

445. Rain forests have four layers: the emergent layer, the canopy, the understory, and the forest floor.

446. The emergent layer is the top layer. The trees here can be between 230 feet (70 meters) and 328 feet (100 meters) tall.

447. The leaves of these tall trees are coated with wax to protect them from the intense heat, heavy rain, and high winds.

448. Because branches at the tops of these trees are thin, only small animals live in the emergent layer.

449. These animals include birds, bats, and small monkeys.

450. Most rain forest trees are in the canopy layer.

451. These trees are about 100 feet (30 meters) tall.

452. About 90 percent of rain forest animals live in the canopy.

453. The understory is very humid and hot.

454. The understory is home to vines, bushes, ferns, climbing plants, and small trees.

455. Many insects live in the understory.

456. The forest floor only receives about 2 percent of the sunlight.

457. Fallen fruit and leaves decay on the forest floor and provide many nutrients.

458. The forest floor is home to large animals, such as tigers, jaguars, and tapirs.

459. Animals that live in the top layers of the rain forest rarely or never come down to the ground.

460. It can take up to 10 minutes for a raindrop to travel from the canopy to the floor.

461. If the Amazon rain forest were a country, it would be the ninth-largest country in the world.

462. A forest has to get between 98 and 177 inches (250 to 450 cm) of rain a year to be called a rain forest.

463. Many ingredients used in modern medicine come from rain forest plants.

464. A 4-square-mile (10-square-km) area of rain forest contains

as many as 1,500 flowering plants, 750 species of trees, 400 species of birds, and 150 species of butterflies.

465. Rain forests are home to 50 percent of the world's plants and animals.

466. About 70 percent of the plants identified by the US National Cancer Institute as useful in the treatment of cancer are found only in rain forests.

467. Scientists have identified more than 2,000 tropical forest plants as having anti-cancer properties.

468. Less than 1 percent of tropical rain forest species have been analyzed for their medicinal value.

469. Between 2000 and 2012, more than 720,000 square miles (2 million square km) of forests around the world were cut down.

470. Rain forests are cut down for ranching, mining, logging, and agriculture.

471. About 80 percent of the natural foods we eat originally came from rain forests.

472. These foods include rice, bananas, potatoes, mangoes, coffee, and cacao.

473. Roughly 20 percent of the world's fresh water supply is located in the Amazon basin.

474. Rain forests are Earth's oldest living ecosystem.

475. They have been around for tens of millions of years.

476. There are 225 species of amphibians in the Amazon rain forest.

477. Rain forests help regulate Earth's weather patterns and temperature.

478. About 50 million indigenous people live in rain forests.

479. There are more freshwater fish in rain forest waterways than anywhere else.

480. Although rain forests are often cleared for agriculture, the land there is not good for farming because the soil has few nutrients.

481. The rain forest is home to many scary and dangerous animals.

482. The green anaconda is the largest snake in the world. It measures up to 30 feet (9 meters) long and weighs more than 500 pounds (227 kg).

483. The Amazon is home to the dangerous bull shark, which can weigh up to 700 pounds (318 kg). This shark eats many different animals and has been known to attack humans.

484. The Amazon's electric eel can still give a nasty shock 8 hours after its death.

485. Poison dart frogs are small, colorful, and deadly. Indigenous people once dipped their blow darts into their poison.

486. The golden poison frog has enough poison to kill 10 men.

# Chapter 4: The beautiful continent

## African Things

487. Africa is bigger than the United States, India, and Canada put together.

488. There are 54 countries and 9 territories on the continent.

489. It is the second-largest continent.

490. Africa is home to more than 1 billion people.

491. Africa's population comprises 15 percent of the world's population.

492. Algeria is the largest country in Africa.

493. Nigeria has the highest population—more than 185 million people.

494. Seychelles is the smallest country, but it is not on the continent. It's a group of islands in the Indian Ocean.

495. The smallest country on the continent is The Gambia.

496. Africa is surrounded by the Atlantic Ocean and the Indian Ocean.

497. Madagascar is Africa's biggest island. It's also the fourth-largest island in the world.

498. The Nile is the longest river in Africa—and in the world. It is 4,258 miles (6,852 meters) long.

499. The Nile has two sources: the White Nile in Tanzania and the Blue Nile in Ethiopia.

500. Mount Kilimanjaro is the highest mountain in Africa. It is 19,340 feet (5,895 meters) tall.

501. Lake Victoria is the largest lake in Africa. It borders Uganda, Tanzania, and Kenya.

502. Lake Victoria is the second-largest freshwater lake in the world. Only Lake Superior in the United States is bigger.

503. Africa's Sahara Desert is the largest hot desert in the world.

504. Sixteen countries in Africa are landlocked. That means none of their territory borders an ocean.

505. There are two tiny countries within the nation of South Africa. They are called Eswatini (formerly Swaziland) and Lesotho.

506. Africa is called "the cradle of humankind." Human life started there about 10 million years ago.

507. Africa had many powerful kingdoms.

508. European nations started colonizing Africa in the 1800s.

509. England, France, Spain, Belgium, Germany, and other countries all had African colonies.

510. Zimbabwe was the last nation to win freedom from Europe. It became independent in 1980.

511. Many colonies changed their names once they became independent.

512. More than 3,000 different native groups live in Africa.

513. About 2,000 different languages are spoken in Africa.

514. In addition to African languages, many people speak English, French, Portuguese, or Arabic.

515. Africa is home to the largest land mammal (elephant), the fastest mammal (cheetah), and the tallest (giraffe).

516. The world's largest reptile is the Nile crocodile.

517. The world's largest primate, the gorilla, lives in Africa.

518. Kruger National Park in South Africa is one of the largest national parks in the world.

519. Visitors to Kruger can see lions, rhinos, leopards, buffaloes, and many more animals.

520. Tugela Falls in South Africa are the continent's highest waterfalls.

521. More than half of Africa is covered by grasslands.

522. There are rain forests in Central Africa.

523. South Africa's Cape Floral Region has the most plant varieties in the world.

524. Africa has about 30 percent of the world's mineral resources.

525. Almost half the gold ever mined came from one place in South Africa.

526. Africa is the world's hottest and second-driest continent.

527. China is Africa's biggest trading partner.

528. Africa and Europe are less than 9 miles (14 km) apart at the Strait of Gibraltar.

529. The world's biggest frog lives in Africa. The Goliath frog grows up to 1 foot (0.3 meter) long and weighs up to 8 pounds (14.5 kg).

530. Ethiopia is the only African country with its own alphabet. Ethiopic is the world's oldest alphabet. And it has 345 letters!

531. Twenty-five percent of the Earth's bird species live in Africa.

532. Over half the population of Africa is under 25 years old. That's the youngest population in the world.

533. Egypt is the most popular tourist destination in Africa.

534. The country of Sudan actually has a lot more pyramids than Egypt does.

535. The name "Africa" comes from the Afri tribe that lived in North Africa.

536. Islam is the largest religion in Africa. Christianity is second largest.

## *Chilly Facts About Antarctica*

537. The South Pole is located in Antarctica.

538. Between 60 and 90 percent of the world's fresh water is locked in Antarctica's ice sheet.

539. If all that ice melted, sea levels would rise about 200 feet (60 meters).

540. In some places, the ice in Antarctica is 2.7 miles (4.5 km) thick.

541. Almost 99 percent of the continent is covered with ice.

542. Antarctica is a desert.

543. The average yearly rainfall at the South Pole is just 0.4 inch (10 mm).

544. If you stand at the South Pole, every direction is north.

545. Antarctica has two active volcanoes.

546. Antarctica is the fifth-largest continent.

547. Blood Falls is a waterfall that stains the ice blood-red.

548. The red color occurs because the water has a high iron contact. When the iron comes in contact with oxygen, it turns red.

549. In 1959, 12 countries signed the Antarctic Treaty. The treaty states that the nations would govern the continent together and it would be reserved for "peace and science."

550. Since 1959, 48 countries have signed the Antarctic Treaty.

551. Antarctica is the only continent that does not have an indigenous, or native, population.

552. No one lives permanently in Antarctica. However, scientists live and work there for part of the year.

553. Penguins and seals are among the animals that live in Antarctica.

554. The name Antarctica comes from a Greek word meaning "opposite of the north."

555. Antarctica isn't just the coldest continent; it is also the windiest.

556. Wind speeds can reach up to 200 miles (320 km) per hour.

557. Antarctica's Gamburtsev Mountains rise up to 9,000 feet (3,000 meters) and are completely covered by more than 15,000 feet (4,572 meters) of ice.

558. Antarctica's Ross Ice Shelf measures 197,000 square miles (510,680 square km).

559. Antarctica wasn't discovered until 1820.

560. Norwegian explorer Roald Amundsen was the first person to reach the South Pole, on December 14, 1911.

561. British explorer Robert Falcon Scott was also trying to be the first person to the South Pole. He arrived just over a month after Amundsen.

562. Scott and his team died on the journey back.

563. Antarctica has only two seasons: winter and summer.

564. The continent has six months of sunlight and six months of darkness.

565. The continent also has about 200 lakes buried under the ice.

566. The largest of these lakes is Lake Vostok. It is covered by 2.5 miles (3.7 km) of solid ice.

## *Amazing Asia*

567. Asia is the largest continent.

568. It covers more than 17 million square miles (44 million square km).

569. That's about one-third of all the land on Earth.

570. Asia has both the highest and lowest points on Earth.

571. It also has the longest coastline.

572. Asia is surrounded by three oceans. the world.

573. About 4.6 billion of the 7.7 billion people in the world live in Asia.

574. China and India both have populations of more than 1 billion people.

575. China has the largest population in

576. Hundreds of different languages are spoken in Asia.

577. The most common are English, Arabic, and Mandarin Chinese.

578. The Caspian Sea is Asia's largest lake.

579. The Caspian Sea's coast touches five different countries.

580. They are Russia, Turkmenistan, Kazakhstan, Azerbaijan, and Iran.

581. The Caspian Sea is one of the deepest lakes in the world at 3,300 feet (1,000 meters).

582. The word Asia may come from the ancient Assyrian word asu, which means "east."

583. Islands make up about 7 percent of Asia's land.

584. Asia's Mount Everest is the tallest mountain in the world. It is 29,035 feet (8,850 meters) high.

585. Mount Everest is part of the Himalayas, which is the highest mountain range in the world.

586. The lowest point on Earth is the Dead Sea, which is 1,410 feet (430 meters) below sea level.

587. Asia's coastline covers about 39,000 miles (62,800 km).

588. All the world's major religions started in Asia.

589. Borneo is the largest island in Asia and the third-largest island in the world.

590. Borneo belongs to three countries: Malaysia, Brunei, and Indonesia.

591. Other large Asian islands include Sumatra, Honshu, and Celebes.

592. Asia includes 48 countries.

593. Russia is the largest country in Asia.

594. Maldives is the smallest.

595. Maldives is a chain of islands. They cover just 116 square miles (300 square km).

596. Asia's longest river is the Yangtze in China.

597. The Yangtze is also called Chang Jiang.

598. It is 3,964 miles (6,380 km) long.

599. Tokyo, Japan, is Asia's largest city.

600. Mongolia's Gobi Desert is the driest place in Asia.

601. Asia has 12 countries with no coastline.

602. They are Uzbekistan, Armenia, Turkmenistan, Kyrgyzstan, Afghanistan, Tajikistan, Laos, Mongolia, Kazakhstan, Nepal, Bhutan, and Azerbaijan.

603. Asia is home to many endangered animals.

604. Many venomous snakes live in Asia.

605. These snakes include the king cobra and the Malayan pit viper.

606. Asia's main natural resources are minerals, oil, and natural gas.

607. Saudi Arabia produces more oil than any other nation.

608. Indonesia is the only Asian country located entirely in the Southern Hemisphere.

609. Some of Earth's oldest civilizations began in Asia.

610. Even though China is one of the world's largest countries, it has only one time zone.

611. Russia has 11 time zones.

612. About 90 percent of the world's rice is eaten in Asia.

613. The highest number of billionaires in the world live in Asia.

614. Nine of the top ten tallest buildings are found in Asia.

615. The ten largest shopping malls in the world are all in Asia.

## *Impressive Famous Places*

616. China›s Great Wall is about 6430 km (3,995 miles) long.

617. There are over 600 rooms in Buckingham Palace.

618. There are seven points on the crown of the Statue of Liberty.

619. New York's Empire State Building weighs more than 365 000 tons.

620. The cherry blossom trees planted along the Tidal Basin were a gift from Tokyo's mayor in 1912.

621. Central Park in New York has more than 225 000 trees.

622. Disneyland was opened in 1955.

623. The Great Pyramid of Giza is the oldest and most intact out of the Ancient Wonders of the World.

624. Before the Eiffel Tower in Paris took the title in 1889, the Washington Monument was the tallest building in the world when it opened in 1884.

625. Since opening in 1805, the Maine Avenue Fish Market has operated continuously, making it the country›s oldest continuously functioning fish market.

626. Georgetown is the city's oldest part, dating back to 1751— 40 years before the founding of Washington, DC.

627. Maine is the only state with a single-syllable name.

628. There are 1,792 stairs at the Eiffel Tower.

629. The bronze statue on top of the U.S. Capitol dome is the Statue of Freedom. It is more than 19 feet tall and weighs nearly 15 000 pounds.

630. The DC War Memorial, which recognizes Washington, DC veterans, is the only memorial on the National Mall dedicated to World War I.

631. Washington, DC is a very international city with more than 175 embassies and cultural centers. Fifteen percent of DC residents speak a language apart from English.

632. The biggest cluster of shopping malls can be found in New Jersey.

633. At Coney Island, New York opened the world›s first roller coaster in 1884.

634. There are 2 500 000 rivets in the Eiffel Tower.

635. To celebrate the friendship between Washington and its sister city Beijing in China, the Friendship Archway over H Street and 7th Street in Chinatown was built in 1986.

636. The full name of Los Angeles is "The People of Our Lady of the City of the Angels of Porciuncula"."

637. Not all White House animals were pets. Woodrow Wilson bought a flock of sheep for grazing on the White House lawn during the First World War. It not only saved the time needed to mow the lawn, but they also sold the wool to collect funds for the Red Cross.

638. At the age of 10, Pablo Picasso enrolled into art school. Barcelona, Spain›s Picasso Museum houses many of his childhood›s «early works.»

639. Although he was meant to be buried at the U.S. Capitol, George Washington willed to be buried at Mount Vernon, his home in Virginia. You can visit his grave during a tour of his estate.

640. The town with the most difficult name is Llanfairpwllgwyngyllgogerychwyrndrobwyll llantysiliogogogoch, and it is located in Wales.

641. Theodore Roosevelt's six children had many pets, including many dogs, a small bear, a lizard, guinea pigs, a pig, a badger, a macaw, a snake, a rooster, a hyena, a barn owl, a rabbit, and Baron Spreckle the hen. He allowed his children to bring their pets to the White House in 1901.

642. The New-York-based Delaware Aquaduct is the world's longest tunnel. It is 137km long and drilled into solid rock.

643. Yellowstone in the US became the first national park in the world in 1872.

# Chapter 5: Encyclopedic knowledge of biology

# Facts About Animals In The Sky

644. The eyes of an eagle are about four times as perceptive than those of a human.

645. Hummingbirds will flap their wings about 200 times a second to hover.

646. The wings of a hummingbird can flap up to 200 times a second.

647. Bats are the only airborne mammals.

648. Pelicans can in a single meal, eat about 1/3 of their body weight.

649. The tawny owl's common' twit-twoo' call comes from a pair of males and females. The key call of the female is the sound of' twit' or' kewick,' while the response of the male is the loud' twoo' or hooting sound.

650. Hummingbirds are the only birds that are able to fly backward.

651. Hummingbirds are unable to walk.

652. Owls are unable to rotate their eyeballs.

653. A chicken›s longest registered flight was 13 seconds.

654. Kiwis scout at night, in the forest floor's leaf carpet. They are the only species of birds that has nostrils in their beaks.

655. The fear of birds is called ornithophobia

656. The teeth of a vampire bat are so sharp that you may not feel the bite at all. Its saliva reduces any feeling, so it could suck its victim's blood for as long as half an hour.

657. Owls are unable to move their eyes from side to side.

658. The tongue of a woodpecker can wrap twice around his head.

659. Birds evolved from theropods.

660. Birds need gravity to swallow, so they will not survive in space.

661. The eye of an ostrich is larger than its brain.

662. There are more than 900 bat species.

663. A hummingbird can beat its wings up to 90 times a second (5400 times a minute).

664. The smallest bird in the world is the 'bee hummingbird' found in Cuba.

665. Thailand's bumblebee bat is the smallest mammal in the world.

666. Pterodactyls were not dinosaurs, but rather airborne reptiles that lived during the dinosaur age. They do not fall into the same group. This also applies to reptiles dependent on water like Plesiosaurs.

667. A woodpecker is able to peck twenty times per second.

668. Flamingos could live up to the age of 80.

# *Proof That Animals Are Weird*

669. The blue whale is the loudest animal alive. It makes a noise that can be heard from over 800 kilometers away.

670. Cows and horses have to sleep while standing up. Can you imagine sleeping while standing?

671. The eggs a shark lays are the biggest eggs in the world!

672. When a hummingbird is hovering in the air, it can beat its wings around 200 times a second.

673. Otters sleep while floating on their backs in the water. They hold each other's hands so they do not float away!

674. The giant squid's eyes are the largest in the entire world.

675. Sharks are the only fish in the ocean that can blink with both their eyes.

676. A crocodile cannot stick its tongue out at you. Its tongue is actually stuck inside its mouth.

677. If you are looking for a shrimp's heart, it is in his head!

678. If you are hiding from a pig, you have to float above him. Pigs actually cannot look up at all.

679. A tiger's skin is striped just like its fur.

680. An ostrich's eye is so big that its brain is smaller than its eye.

681. A gorilla can get sick, just like humans can.

682. Bats are the only mammals on Earth that can fly!

683. Speaking of bats, they cannot walk because their leg bones are too thin.

684. A tarantula, which is a big, friendly spider, can survive up to two years without eating any food.

685. Kangaroos use their tails for balance; if you lift their tail up off the ground it will not be able to hop.

686. You know cows can sleep while standing. Well, they can only have dreams if they are lying down.

687. For every one human in the world, there are about one million ants.

688. Also, the weight of all the ants in the world would match the weight of all the humans in the world.

689. A goldfish gets its orange color from light. If you keep one in a dark room, it will turn into a pale fish!

690. Alligators can be really old. They can live for up to 100 years.

691. An elephant's tooth can weigh up to nine pounds. That is quite a heavy tooth!

692. Can you eat while hanging upside down? A flamingo cannot eat unless its head is upside down.

693. An anteater's mouth is only an inch wide. No wonder it cannot eat anything but ants.

694. Ants never get tired and they never sleep.

695. Speaking of ants, they do not have any lungs!

696. Horses run fast, but an ostrich can run faster than a horse.

697. Also, the male ostrich can roar just like a lion does.

698. In green areas, like forests and fields, every acre contains about 50,000 spiders!

699. The blue-eyed lemur is one of only two primates that are not human to have eyes that are truly blue.

700. A blue whale can weigh the same as 30 fully grown elephants.

701. A skunk smells so bad that you can smell it from up to a mile away!

702. There is one species of butterfly that lives in Africa that is so poisonous it can kill up to six cats!

703. A snake can see you even with its eyes closed because it can actually see through its eyelids.

704. A hummingbird is so good at flying that it can even fly backward.

705. A rhino's horn is not made of bone. It is made out of compacted hair.

706. Sheep have four stomachs! Each one helps them digest their food, but humans only need one.

707. Cows also have four stomachs. They need each one to help them digest their food.

708. Polar bears' fur might look white, but it is actually transparent.

709. Speaking of polar bears, their skin is completely black, but you cannot see it underneath the fur.

710. Most people are killed by more crocodiles than lions in Africa.

711. Cats' whiskers are used to check if they can fit into or through something. If their whiskers are too wide, they know they will not fit!

712. Bees do not look like they fly very fast, but a bee can fly up to 15 miles per hour!

713. A shark's skeleton is made out of cartilage, not bone like ours.

714. Elephants are the largest mammals on land in the whole world.

715. A giraffe only has seven bones in its neck! That is the same amount of bones a human has in their neck.

716. Frogs do not drink water; they soak it in through the skin!

717. Dogs have better hearing than humans. Their hearing is four times stronger than ours.

718. Dolphins are carnivores! (That means they eat meat.)

719. An elephant needs to drink at least 210 liters of water a day.

720. Cats are very lazy. They can sleep between 13 and 14 hours a day!

721. A wolf is the ancestor of all the breeds of domestic dogs in the world.

722. Wolves are also part of the animal group called "wild dogs," which includes coyotes and dingoes. All dogs came from this group of animals at first.

723. Dolphins breathe through the blowhole on the top of their head!

724. A giraffe's tongue is a blueish purple color, and it is covered in long bristles.

725. Speaking of giraffes, the bristles on a giraffe's tongue help it eat thorny plants.

726. Frogs can see in front of them, above them, and on the side of them, all at the same time!

727. Turtles can actually breathe using their butts!

728. Cheetahs are so nervous that some zoos give them support dogs.

729. Humpback whales will let dolphins ride on their backs for fun.

730. A hippopotamus' skin is 1.5 inches thick.

731. Flamingos are bright pink because of the color of the food they eat.

732. Giraffes are the only animals in the whole world that cannot yawn.

733. A bee needs to use 22 muscles to sting!

734. Cats cannot taste anything that is sweet.

735. Spiders' blood is transparent, which means it is clear like water.

736. Snails move so slow it will take them 115 days to travel only a mile.

737. Dolphins' brains are actually bigger than a human's brain.

738. Dolphins are also considered to be the most intelligent animals on the planet.

739. A rat cannot vomit!

740. Elephants are the only mammals on Earth that cannot jump.

741. Rattlesnakes are still able to bite you for up to an hour after they die; this is because of their reflex actions.

742. A pigeon's feathers will weigh more than its bones do!

743. The great horned owl is the only animal in existence that will eat a skunk.

744. If you put an electric eel in salt water, it will short-circuit itself. They need to live in fresh water.

745. In a goat's eye, the pupil is a rectangular shape.

746. A crocodile's bite is the strongest bite in the world! It is 12 times stronger than a great white shark's bite.

747. Some animals, such as frogs and fish, can be frozen completely during winter and then unfreeze in spring and be completely unharmed and healthy.

748. If a shark swims upside down, it could slip into a coma!

749. Giraffes' tongues are over 18 inches long, and they use their tongues to clean their ears.

750. A newborn baby kangaroo is so small that it could fit inside a teaspoon.

751. A koala bear is so lazy it needs to sleep about 22 hours a day!

752. An earthworm has so much love because it has up to nine hearts.

753. A tiger can be trained to use a litter box just like a normal cat.

754. A single beaver can cut down up to 200 trees in a year with its teeth.

755. Mosquitoes are attracted to the color blue; they really love it!

756. When a penguin falls in love, they will search the whole beach for the perfect pebble to give to the penguin that they love.

757. Penguins mate for life! They choose one partner to fall in love with and stay with them for their entire lives.

758. Penguins also have an organ in their eyes that turn salt water into fresh water.

759. Penguins can also stay underwater for up to 27 minutes.

760. Dolphins communicate with each other using whistling, clicking, and other sounds. Each dolphin can actually develop its own unique sound.

761. The buzzing noise that most insects, such as bees and mosquitoes, make is caused by the rapid movement of their wings.

762. Americans tried to train bats to drop bombs during World War II.

763. If you place even a tiny amount of alcohol on a scorpion it will be driven crazy and sting itself.

764. A female rabbit is called a "doe" and a male rabbit is called a "buck."

765. A female elephant can be pregnant for up to two whole years.

766. Lobsters and jellyfish are considered to be immortal. Unless killed by something in their environment, they will never die.

767. Wild parrots are able to name their children, and that name sticks for life, just like humans.

768. Monkeys, koala bears, and humans are the only animals on Earth that have unique, individual fingerprints.

## Dark Facts About Nocturnal Animals

769. Nocturnal animals have big eyes to help them see in the dark.

770. An owl's eyes are so big, they can't move within their sockets.

771. A cat's eyes have a special layer called a tapetum that reflects light. That's why their eyes glow in the dark.

772. Many nocturnal animals have a slit pupil in their eye. A slit pupil can open and close quickly when light changes.

773. Bioluminescent animals produce their own light.

774. Some fish are bioluminescent.

775. Fireflies are also bioluminescent.

776. Bioluminescent animals create light to communicate with each other.

777. They also use their light to locate food and attract prey.

778. Bioluminescent animals can flash their lights to scare away predators.

779. Bats use sound to find food. They make high-pitched squeaks that bounce off objects.

780. This process is called echolocation.

781. An owl's hearing is so sharp it can hear tiny animals rustling in the grass.

782. Lions hunt at night because it is cooler then.

783. Lions also hunt at night because their prey—zebra and antelopes—have poor night vision.

784. Sea turtles breed in the dark to avoid predators. They come out of the sea to lay their eggs on the beach.

785. Sea birds also breed at night to stay safe.

786. Many fish are active during the night.

787. When it is dark, it is easier for fish to see the tiny zooplankton they eat.

788. Bats and bush babies are only able to see at night.

789. Because scents linger on the night air, it is easier for animals to smell and track prey at night.

790. Owls have special feathers that help them fly very quietly. Their prey never hears them coming!

791. Aardvarks can hear and smell insects as they walk around.

792. Fewer animals hunt at night than during the day, so nocturnal hunters have less competition.

793. Some nocturnal animals, such as foxes, can also be seen during the day.

794. About 80 percent of marsupials and 60 percent of carnivores are nocturnal.

795. About 40 percent of rodents and 20 percent of primates are nocturnal.

796. Animals that are active at dawn and dusk are called crepuscular.

797. Both wild cats and pet cats have ears that can move. This helps them locate sounds in the dark.

798. A cat's cupped ear shape helps it take in more sound.

799. Some nocturnal animals can hear separately with each ear. This helps them pinpoint where a sound is coming from.

800. All eyes contain rods and cones. Rods are better at collecting low light.

801. Nocturnal animals' eyes have more rods than animals active during the day.

802. Cones work well in bright light. Nocturnal snakes, lizards, and bats do not have any cones in their eyes.

803. Activity is regulated by a person or animal's circadian rhythm. This rhythm is regulated by light cues.

804. Light signals diurnal (active during the day) animals to wake up and be active.

805. In nocturnal animals, light signals it is time to go to sleep.

806. Zoos often exhibit nocturnal animals in dark rooms so they will be active for daytime visitors to see.

807. Most species of spiders are nocturnal.

808. Many amphibians and reptiles are nocturnal.

809. Nocturnal animals usually hide during the day.

810. Nocturnal salamanders bury themselves in mud.

811. Other nocturnal animals hide under rocks or leaves.

812. Amphibians need to stay wet. Nights are usually more humid than days, so being nocturnal helps these animals survive.

813. Mosquitoes are active at night because it is cooler then. Too much sun can kill them.

# Chapter 6: Our Diet

## Foodies Need To Know

814. Two-thirds of the world's eggplants are grown in New Jersey in the United States.

815. Rice is the staple food for 50% of the population globally.

816. Cucumbers are in fact fruit and are part of the melon family.

817. Apples float in water!

818. Italy has twenty regions, each with its own special cuisine. Dishes made in Rome, may not be popular in Florence. Thus, there is no such thing as Italian food.

819. Coffee is typically roasted between 204-218C (400-425F) (the longer the roasting of the beans, the darker the roast).

820. Before they were orange, carrots used to be only purple.

821. Roasting coffee beans burns off caffeine, so dark roasted coffee beans contain less caffeine than medium roasted ones.

822. Once upon a time, ice cream was called cream ice.

823. Tomatoes are not indigenous to Italy; they were imported from the Americas.

824. Apart from Antarctica, corn is cultivated on every continent.

825. The Snickers Bar was created by Franklin Mars in 1930.

826. The fear of having peanut butter sticking to your palate is called arachibutyrophobia.

827. 7% of the U.S. population consumes McDonalds on a daily basis.

828. The original name for Cheerios cereal was Cheerioats.

829. The only fruit with its seed on the outside is the strawberry.

830. 52 percent of Americans are coffee drinkers.

831. Cucumbers consist of 96% water.

832. Pound cake got its name because of the ingredients which are a pound of butter, a pound of sugar, a pound of eggs and a pound of flour.

833. Of all the pineapples, more than a third comes from Hawaii.

834. The average American diet is 55% junk food.

835. In Denmark, 93% of households drink wine (the highest percentage of households in the world with France second with 85%).

836. It takes two years for a pineapple to mature.

837. The longest French fry in the world measured 34 inches long.

838. Coffee accounts for 75% of all caffeine drunk in the U.S.

839. The smallest fruit in the world— a utricle— is the same size as a tiny ant.

840. Cherries, quince, pears, plums, strawberries, peaches and raspberries all belong to the rose family (Rosaceae).

841. Pasta was a finger food before pasta sauce was invented. Since the sauce-free pasta was eaten by hand, no forks were required.

842. They first launched frozen foods in the 1920s.

843. The larger the orange, the sweeter it is.

844. The number one food craved by women is chocolate.

845. There are very high levels of antioxidants in blueberries.

846. Ripe cranberries can bounce and they can also float.

847. There are more than 15 000 different varieties of rice.

848. 22% of all restaurant meals usually have potato chips.

849. Tomato Sauce was first documented in the history of food in the late 18th century.

850. Vanilla is America's best-selling ice cream flavor.

851. Pizza originated in Naples in 1889.

852. The world's largest seed was made by the double coconut palm, it weighed 45 pounds.

853. Garlic bulbs are filled with vitamin C, copper, potassium, magnesium, zinc, etc. It has 17 amino acids as well.

854. Almonds and peaches are from the same class.

855. The favorite green vegetable in the world is lettuce.

856. You can buy banana beer in eastern Africa.

857. Some apples can weigh almost the same as half a gallon of milk.

858. On average, Italians eat half a pound of bread every day.

859. The popular "Caprese" appetizer (made of mozzarella, tomatoes, and basil) is called "Insalata Caprese" because a chef on the island of Capri made it.

860. Yearly pasta consumption in Italy is thought to be 70 pounds per person.

861. Dairy products make up 29% of all food consumed in the United States.

## The Knowledge of Eating

862. The most expensive pizza in the world is known to take around 72 hours to make and is made by three private chefs in your home. It costs $12,000 for just one pizza.

863. Ranch dressing is dyed using titanium dioxide, which is also used in sunscreen and paint, in order to make it appear whiter.

864. Nutmeg contains a compound called "myristicin." If you eat a large amount of nutmeg, this compound will make you hallucinate.

865. The pound cake is called that because its original recipe called for a pound of eggs, a pound of butter, and a pound of sugar.

866. Most fruit-flavored snacks have a shine on them, and this shine is caused by carnauba wax, which is also used on cars.

867. Just one burger from a fast-food restaurant can contain meat from 100 different cows.

868. Ketchup was used as medicine in the early 1800s. It was believed that it could treat indigestion and diarrhea.

869. During this time in the 1800s, there was a special recipe that was used to turn ketchup into a pill.

870. Crackers have holes in them because the holes stop air bubbles from forming while the crackers are baking. This prevents the crackers from being ruined.

871. The burn you feel from chili peppers is fake. A chemical called "capsaicin" tricks your mouth into feeling the burn from spicy food.

872. White chocolate does not contain any of the components used in actual chocolate, which means that it is not actually chocolate.

873. The first ice cream cone was introduced to the world in 1904.

874. Crackers cause more damage to your teeth than sugar does.

875. Wild salmon are pink because they eat shrimp. Farmed salmon do not eat shrimp so they are white. Before selling them, the farmers dye the salmon pink.

876. In Russia, until 2013, alcoholic beverages containing 10% or less alcohol, such as beer, were actually not considered alcoholic. They were considered soft drinks!

877. The beetle called "Dactylopius coccus" is crushed and boiled in order to produce the red tint on most strawberry, cherry, and raspberry flavored candy, such as the red Skittles.

878. Processed cheese is also known as American cheese, but it was actually first made in Switzerland.

879. Speaking of cheese, it is the most stolen food in the world! Around 4% of the world's cheese ends up stolen.

880. Chocolate is so good that it was once used as currency by different civilizations in South America and Mexico.

881. Peanut oil is used when making dynamite!

882. The expiration date on water bottles is not for the water but for the actual bottle.

883. Water can never expire, so ignore the "best by" date!

884. "Arachibutyrophobia" is the name for the fear of peanut butter, specifically the fear of getting it stuck to the roof of your mouth.

885. Honey is actually bee vomit!

886. Nutella uses up about 25% of the world's hazelnuts. One out of every four hazelnuts will end up in a jar of Nutella.

887. Studies have shown that listening to loud music can make you drink faster and drink more.

888. The Froot Loops cereal might be made of all different colors, but they all actually taste the same.

889. It can take between 144 to 411 licks to reach the center of a tootsie pop, with the average amount of licks being 364.

890. French fries are not actually French; they were first made in Belgium.

891. During ancient Egyptian times, workers were paid with garlic, radishes, and onions, with radishes being the favorite.

892. A pineapple technically is not known as a fruit. It is a bunch of berries that have fused together to form one giant berry.

893. Strawberries cannot be considered berries because usually berries only have seeds on the inside.

894. Pineapples have nothing to do with pine or pine trees. When they were first discovered, they were thought to looked like a pine cone.

895. Chefs in Japan have to be trained for more than two years before they can serve someone a pufferfish.

896. If someone eats pufferfish that is not prepared properly, it can kill them.

897. The cream in the center of a Twinkie is not actually cream. It is vegetable shortening.

898. No one knows where the first recipe for chocolate chip cookies came from, although there are several theories.

899. It is thanks to Thomas Jefferson that pasta is famous in the United States. He spent some time in France and brought a macaroni machine back to the United States with him.

900. Thomas Jefferson is also responsible for introducing Americans to mac and cheese.

901. Cauliflower comes in many different colors, including purple, green, and orange, though we typically only see the white variety.

902. The Margherita pizza is named after Queen Margherita. She loved it so much after eating it during her visit to Naples with her husband King Umberto I.

903. If you place eggs in water, the rotten eggs will float, and the fresh ones will sink.

904. Raw lima beans have enough cyanide in them to kill you. However, if the lima beans are properly cooked, then they are safe to eat.

905. Not all wine is vegan. Some wines contain egg whites, milk protein, gelatin, and sometimes even fish bladder protein.

906. If you want to know if a cranberry is ripe, drop it to the ground. Ripe cranberries will bounce like a ball.

907. According to the FDA, there is actually an allowance for insects in food products.

908. The popsicle was invented by accident when an 11-year-old boy left some water and soda in a cup overnight to freeze.

909. In the country of China, bird saliva is considered to be known as a delicacy. There is a dish called "Bird's Nest Soup."

910. Chewing on coffee beans can get rid of bad breath.

911. Food will taste different in an airplane than it does on the ground. This is because a higher altitude changes your body's chemistry.

912. Orange juice is one of the main ingredients in Mountain Dew.

913. The name "Chimichanga," given to a type of food, actually means "thingamajig."

914. Humans share 60% of our DNA with bananas!

915. Potatoes are made up of up to 80% water.

916. Turkey sure does love tea. They consume the most tea per person in the world. That is almost seven pounds of tea a year.

917. Tonic water can actually glow in the dark!

918. There is a difference between jam and jelly. Jelly is made with fruit juice while jam is made with fruit.

919. India consumes the least amount of meat in the whole world.

920. Due to the reproductive process of a wasp, figs may contain the decomposed body of a wasp.

921. The country of India is known to be the largest producer and consumer of chili peppers in the whole world.

922. Around 49% of all Americans over the age of 20 eat at least one sandwich every day.

923. Pule cheese, which is made from donkey milk in Serbia, is the most expensive cheese in the world. It costs over $1,000 per pound.

924. Before kale became popular around 2010, Pizza Hut purchased the most kale out of the whole nation, and they only used it as a garnish at their salad bars.

925. Each person in the Netherlands drinks about 2.5 cups of coffee a day. That is the most in the world.

926. Nutritious food costs up to ten times more than junk food.

927. Fortune cookies were invented in San Francisco in the early 1900s, and they are not Chinese.

928. It is so cold in the Arctic that people use refrigerators to stop their food from freezing.

929. It is illegal to throw food away in Seattle, Washington.

930. Up to 40% of the produce that is grown does not get sold simply because it is too ugly.

931. Sound actually changes how food tastes. High frequency makes things sweeter, whereas low frequency makes things more bitter.

932. Opposite to India, Australians eat the most meat out of the whole world.

933. Americans eat 500 million pounds of peanut butter a year.

934. It does not matter how hot it is outside; you cannot cook an egg on the sidewalk.

935. "Breakfast is the most important meal of the day" was a lie used by a company called General Foods to sell more cereal.

936. You can find traces of wood pulp inside shredded cheese.

937. The German chocolate cake is not German and has nothing to do with Germany. It was invented by a Texan using German chocolate, which is only called that because of its creator, Sam German.

938. Coriander and cilantro are not the same thing. Cilantro is the plant's leaves and stems, whereas coriander is the dried seeds.

939. The pecan nut is Alabama's state nut. They have a pecan festival each year!

940. Breast milk is the only food in existence that can provide you with all the nutrients your body needs. You could survive off of drinking it alone and nothing else.

941. Enough Nutella is sold each year to cover The Great Wall of China eight times.

942. There are about 15,000 Indian restaurants in London. That is more than there are in Delhi or Mumbai.

943. The Margherita pizza was originally made to match the colors of the Italian flag.

944. The first food grown in space was red romaine lettuce, and it was eaten by astronauts in 2015.

945. California is in the top five out of all the food producers in the whole world.

946. Goat meat is the most popular meat eaten in the world. Approximately 70% of the world's red meat is goat meat.

947. If you do not eat food before going to bed, your body will burn more fat while you sleep.

948. It would take you 20 years to eat all of the varieties of apples even if you ate an apple a day.

949. Cotton candy, which is famously known for being bad for your teeth, was co-created by a dentist.

950. About 70% of the spice in the world comes from India.

951. Pizza Hut once delivered a pizza to the top of Kilimanjaro, which is the record for the highest pizza delivery in the world.

952. You should keep your bananas separate from the rest of your fruit because bananas make other fruits go bad faster.

953. A study was conducted that proved that hot chocolate tastes better out of an orange cup.

954. A year after opening Domino's pizza, James Monaghan, the co-founder, traded his half of the company for a used VW Beetle.

955. 38 years after the opening of Domino's pizza, Tom Monaghan, the other co-founder, sold his share of the company for $1 billion.

956. Cow's milk can turn pink if the cow eats too many carrots.

957. There is a blue banana called the Blue Java banana that has a vanilla taste.

958. Spaghetti is the plural form of the word. Spaghetto is the singular form.

959. The Galmburger is the most expensive burger in the world, and it costs $1,768.

960. Salt was worth its weight in gold during Roman times. Roman soldiers were often paid with salt.

961. There is a plant called a "Pomato," which can produce both tomatoes and potatoes.

# Chapter 7: Impressive Geography

# Rocks, Minerals, And Gems

962. Rocks and minerals are not the same thing.

963. A mineral is a naturally occurring inorganic (nonliving) element.

964. A rock is made up of at least two minerals.

965. Rocks can also include fossils.

966. Scientists who study rocks and minerals are called geologists.

967. A rock is bigger than a pebble but smaller than a boulder.

968. There are three types of rocks.

969. Igneous rocks are formed by volcanoes.

970. There are over 700 types of igneous rocks, such as basalt, pumice, granite, and obsidian.

971. There are two kinds of igneous rocks: extrusive and intrusive, depending on whether they formed inside or outside of a volcano.

972. Extrusive igneous rocks form when magma cools and hardens outside a volcano. They often look like shiny glass.

973. Intrusive igneous rocks form inside the Earth. They often look rough.

974. Metamorphic rocks are made by great pressure inside the Earth.

975. Sedimentary rocks are layers of sediment (dirt and mud) pressing together and turning into stone.

976. Rocks can change from one type to another. This is called the rock cycle.

977. Igneous rocks can break down into sediment. Then they can form sedimentary rocks.

978. Sedimentary rocks can move deep into the Earth's crust. Pressure can then turn them into metamorphic rocks.

979. Meteorites are rocks that came here from space. They are mostly made of iron.

980. The word igneous comes from the Latin "ignis," which means "fire."

981. Mohs Scale of Hardness measures how hard or soft a mineral is.

982. A mineral with a higher number can scratch a mineral with a lower number.

983. Talc is #1 on the scale. It is the softest mineral.

984. Diamonds are #10. They are the hardest and can scratch any other mineral.

985. Minerals are judged by seven different properties. They are: crystal form, hardness, fracture, luster, color, streak, and density.

986. There are more than 4,000 different types of minerals.

987. Jade was a royal gem in ancient China.

988. Ancient civilizations believed gems and minerals had magical powers.

989. People have used rocks for millions of years.

990. Rocks can be weapons, tools, or building material.

991. Pumice is an unusual igneous rock. It forms when it is blasted out of a volcano. Pumice is very light because it is full of air holes.

992. Marble is a metamorphic rock formed from the sedimentary rock limestone.

993. Chalk is a soft form of limestone.

994. Limestone is made of seashells and the bodies of tiny sea creatures.

995. The atoms in a mineral are arranged in a specific pattern. This is called crystallization.

996. Fossils are usually found in sedimentary rocks.

997. The layers in a sedimentary rock are called strata.

998. Minerals are found in soap, detergent, toothpaste, and much more.

999. Ninety-five percent of the Earth's crust is made of igneous rock.

1000. The biggest nugget of pure gold was found in Australia in 1869. It weighed 156 pounds (71 kg).

1001. A gem is a mineral that has been cut and polished.

1002. Gemstones are measured in carats.

1003. A carat weighs 200 milligrams, or .00643 troy ounce.

1004. The minerals in a gem determine its color.

1005. Diamonds are the most valuable gems.

1006. Amber is the softest gem.

1007. The largest diamond found in the United States was the Uncle Sam Diamond.

1008. It was found in Arkansas in 1924.

1009. The Uncle Sam Diamond weighs more than 40 carats.

1010. Quartz comes in more colors than any other gem. Quartz can be purple, yellow, brown, pink, or a mix of colors.

1011. Granite makes up a large part of the continents.

1012. The sea floor is made of an igneous rock called basalt.

1013. Basalt is hardened lava.

1014. Some granite rocks in Australia are believed to be more than 4 billion years old.

1015. Gemstones were mined in ancient Egypt.

1016. Gemstones are graded by the 4 C's: color, clarity, cut, and carat weight.

## Cave Facts To Explore

1017. Caves form when water flows over soft rock.

1018. Acid in the water eats away at the rock.

1019. Many caves are made of a soft rock called limestone.

1020. Caves can also form when hot lava melts rocks and creates holes.

1021. Tidal waters on the coast can carve caves out of rocks on the shore.

1022. Caves take between 10,000 and 100,000 years to form.

1023. The study of caves is called speleology.

1024. Caves can also be called caverns.

1025. Caves are completely dark inside.

1026. Some caves have hanging pieces called stalactites.

1027. Stalactites form when water drips from the ceiling. The lime in the water hardens and creates stalactites.

1028. Stalagmites are hardened minerals that rise from the floor of a cave.

1029. Stalactites and stalagmites can join together to form columns.

1030. Sheets of hardened lime on cave walls are called flowstones.

1031. Caves can have many long passageways and rooms.

1032. Exploring caves is called spelunking.

1033. Exploring is also called caving and potholing.

1034. Caves provide shelter for many animals.

1035. Some species of bats live deep inside caves.

1036. Bats are trogloxenes. That means they live in caves part of the time.

1037. Troglobites are animals that live deep inside caves and never go outside.

1038. Blind cave fish have no eyes. They don't need to see in the dark.

1039. Treasures and artifacts from ancient times have been found inside caves.

1040. The Kruber-Voronya Cave in the Asian country of Georgia is the world's deepest cave. It is 7,208 feet (2,197 meters) deep.

1041. The largest cave in the world is Son Doong in Vietnam.

1042. Son Doong covers 1.35 billion cubic feet (38.5 cubic meters).

1043. In 2019, divers discovered that Son Doong is connected to another huge cave called Hang Thung.

1044. There are about 17,000 caves in the United States.

1045. Rhode Island and Louisiana are the only states that do not have caves.

1046. The largest cave in the United States is Mammoth Cave in Kentucky.

1047. It is also the longest cave in the world.

1048. About 365 miles (587 km) of Mammoth Cave have been mapped so far.

1049. Most of Mammoth Cave was mapped by enslaved explorers and guides in the 1800s.

1050. Many caves are filled with water. Some have rivers running through them.

1051. If you discover a new cave, you get to name it.

1052. The Great Blue Hole off the coast of Belize is a 400-foot (122-meter)-deep sinkhole.

1053. The Great Blue Hole is a favorite spot for scuba diving.

1054. It is also home to several species of sharks and tropical fish.

1055. New Mexico's Carlsbad Caverns includes more than 100 caves.

1056. Missouri is called the Cave State because it contains more than 6,000 caves.

# Explosive Knowledge About Volcanic Eruptions

1057. The deadliest eruption in recent history was Mt. Tambora in Indonesia.

1058. Mt. Tambora erupted in 1815 and killed as many as 120,000 people.

1059. The eruption sent volcanic ash 25 miles (40 km) into the sky.

1060. Tambora's eruption caused the global temperature to drop and led to crop failures around the world.

1061. When Krakatoa erupted in Indonesia in 1883, it completely destroyed the island it sat on.

1062. Krakatoa's eruption has been called the loudest sound in history.

1063. The eruption could be heard thousands of miles (km) away.

1064. Krakatoa's eruption and the following tsunamis killed more than 36,000 people.

1065. When a volcano named Laki erupted in Iceland in 1783, toxic gases poisoned crops and killed more than half of Iceland's livestock.

1066. It also killed more than 10,000 people in Iceland.

1067. Toxic gases traveled to Great Britain and killed another 23,000 people.

1068. The Laki eruption lasted for eight months.

1069. People thought the Mt. Pele volcano on the island of Martinique was dormant. They were wrong.

1070. Mt. Pele erupted in 1902, burying the city of Saint Pierre and killing more than 28,000 people.

1071. Only two people in Saint Pierre survived. One was a prisoner locked in an underground cell.

1072. The eruption also capsized 15 ships in the harbor.

1073. It was the most powerful eruption in the twentieth century.

1074. Japan's deadliest volcanic eruption was Mt. Unzen in 1792.

1075. The eruption caused a landslide that buried the city of Shimabara.

1076. When the landslide flowed into the ocean, it created tsunami waves 187 feet (57 meters) high.

1077. The Mt. Unzen eruption killed about 15,000 people.

1078. Colombia's Nevada del Ruiz eruption caused a mudslide that killed 20,000 people.

1079. Nevada del Ruiz caused $1 billion in damages, making it the most expensive volcano eruption.

1080. The second-largest eruption in the twentieth century was Mt. Pinatubo in the Philippines.

1081. The 1991 eruption left 200,000 people homeless.

1082. When Mt. Vesuvius erupted in Italy in the year 79, it buried the cities of Pompeii and Herculaneum.

# Chapter 8: Time And Space

## *Impressive Things of Time*

1083. There was a war that only lasted for 38 minutes, and it is the shortest war in history.

1084. 10,000 years was the longest jail sentence ever passed.

1085. The bacteria in your ear are increased by 700 times if you wear headphones for an hour.

1086. "Planck time" is the name given to the smallest scientific measure of time.

1087. Oxford University has been around longer than the Aztecs.

1088. Our universe is around 13.8 billion years old.

1089. The International Fixed Calendar has 13 months instead of 12.

1090. A year contains a total of 31,557,600 seconds.

1091. In 63 years, humans progressed from taking our first airplane flight to landing on the moon.

1092. There is a clock called the "Strontium Atomic Clock," and it is the most accurate teller of time ever built.

1093. There is a clock that uses the position of the sun to measure time by casting a shadow. It is called a "sundial."

1094. Julius Caesar invented the leap year in 46 B.C.

1095. The first modern clock was invented in 1511 by a man named Peter Henle.

1096. 1,000,000,000,000 years is called a "gigayear."

1097. The longest eclipse of the sun that is possible is about 7.31 minutes long.

1098. The time zone that the International Space Station follows is GMT.

1099. Julius Caesar created the Julian calendar, which was based around the earth's rotations around the sun.

1100. An average human will blink around 25,000 times a day.

1101. Russia, the largest country of the world, has to use up to 11 consecutive time zones.

1102. During the Mesozoic Era, when dinosaurs were still roaming the earth, a year contained about 370 days.

1103. Alaska and Hawaii, although really far away from one another, have the same time zone.

1104. The study of devices that are used to measure time and the scientific study of time itself is called "Horology."

1105. Greenland is known as the world's largest island, and it has to use four different time zones.

1106. It takes the moon 27.32 days to fully orbit the earth.

1107. The idea of Daylight Saving was first proposed by Benjamin Franklin, although his proposal was a similar solution but not actually Daylight Saving.

1108. Daylight Saving is when we have to turn all the clocks forward by an hour in order to keep the correct time.

1109. The Sunday that comes directly after the first full moon after the Spring Equinox is known as "Easter."

1110. If you spend a year at the top of Mount Everest, it would be 15 microseconds shorter than a year spent at sea level.

1111. The continent of Australia needs to have both a vertical and a horizontal time zone during the summer.

1112. China has been divided into five time zones because it is so big.

1113. A study showed that most serial killers are more likely to be born in November.

1114. We all know that February has 28 days, except during a leap year when it has 29 days. Did you know that February 30th has been an actual day in history?

1115. Kissing someone for an entire minute burns around 26 calories.

1116. It takes around 550 thousand trillion, trillion, trillion Planck seconds to blink once.

1117. Einstein once said that there was no distinction between the past, present, and future because they are all an illusion.

1118. Time does not actually exist. It is just a concept that we all agree on in order to keep track of the days.

1119. During the last ice age, beavers were as large as bears.

1120. 3:44 in the morning is the average time people usually wake up for no apparent reason at all.

1121. Humans first started eating cooked food as far back as 1.9 million years ago.

1122. Around 400 million years ago, the earth was covered in 24-foot mushrooms instead of trees.

1123. If you are angry for a minute, it weakens your immune system for up to four or five hours.

1124. Time moves slower for animals like chipmunks, hummingbirds, and other small rodents.

1125. A day does not last 24 hours. It takes the earth 23 hours, 56 minutes, and 4.2 seconds to rotate one time.

1126. There is a crystal that is 4.4 billion years old, and it is considered the oldest object on Earth. It is only 160 million years younger than the earth itself.

1127. It takes time for light from objects, such as the sun and the stars, to reach us. In other words, the light that we see is already in the past.

1128. The saying "Time flies when you are having fun" is actually not true. Research shows that time actually slows down when you are enjoying yourself.

1129. We know that the universe began around 15 billion years ago with the big bang, but we have no idea exactly when the universe will end.

1130. The sun has been around for five billion years while Earth has been around for about 4.5 billion years.

1131. In Russia, weekends were abolished in 1931 to improve productivity. They went back to a seven-day week only in 1941.

1132. There are whales in the ocean with 200-year-old ivory spear tips still lodged in their flesh.

1133. The average human's heart beats around 100,000 times a day.

1134. China made up 33% of the world's GDP in 1820. Today, it only makes up around 4.5%.

1135. The first calendar only contained ten months and started in March. It was based on the phases of the moon.

1136. The Roman calendar did not assign a specific month to winter. This made the whole year 304 days long with 61 of those days making up winter.

1137. Julius Caesar, a well-known Roman general and statesmen, was the one that introduced the months of July, named after him, and August, named after his successor.

1138. In 2011, there was a study done that showed four babies were being born every second of every day.

1139. The same study showed that two people die every second of every day.

1140. By the time the average human turns 70 years old, their heart will have beaten around 2.5 billion times.

1141. In the year 1836, a man named John Belville used to charge people money to tell them what time it was.

1142. If a lightning strike is seen at least three seconds before thunder is heard, it means that the lightning strike happened about 0.6 miles away.

1143. The Sumerians were the first civilization in history known to keep track of time and have a calendar of their own.

1144. During the 16th century B.C., people in Babylon kept time using bowls filled with water.

1145. A person who sleeps an average of eight hours a night will sleep around 229,961 hours during their lifetime.

1146. The longest time spent playing a board game is 80 hours!

1147. According to the laws of physics, the faster you move, the slower time moves around you. If you moved faster, you would live longer.

1148. The day of April 11th, 1954 is known as the day when nothing happened.

1149. We call ten years a "decade," 100 years a "century," and finally, 1,000 years a "millennium."

1150. The moon was used to create calendars around 6,000 years ago.

1151. The number of blinks the average human has a day is equivalent to having your eyes closed for about 30 minutes.

1152. The average human has hiccups for around five minutes.

1153. Niagara Falls has so much water that it could fill a bathtub every second.

1154. A hummingbird's wings flap around 90 times a second.

1155. It takes less time for dirty snow to melt than it does for clean snow.

1156. The human body sheds all of its skin every four weeks.

1157. A moment actually lasts around one minute and 30 seconds. This is according to the old English time system.

1158. The most common time for humans to wake up is 7 a.m.

1159. A person was once in a coma for 37 years, and that is the longest time anyone has been in a coma.

1160. A housefly has a reaction time of 30 milliseconds, which is why it is difficult to swat one.

1161. A tree does not have a life expectancy. If unaffected by nature or man, a tree will continue to grow for eternity.

1162. A container made of plastic will take an average of 50,000 years to start decomposing.

1163. There is a name for a 15th anniversary. It is called a "quindecennial."

1164. A nanosecond is the equivalent of one billionth of a second.

1165. Sharks are one of the oldest animals on Earth. They have been known to have existed here for over 400 million years.

1166. The Stonehenge in England is only around 5,000 years old.

1167. The average human can go a few weeks without food, but they will die after ten days without sleep.

1168. During the 1900s in the United States, the average lifespan was around 47 years.

1169. The average human will produce enough saliva to fill two average-sized swimming pools in their lifetime.

1170. It would take you about 193 years to drive to the sun if you were driving at a constant 55 miles per hour.

1171. It takes a cheetah only three seconds to go from zero miles per hour to 43 miles per hour.

1172. We have found fossils of cockroaches that are over 280 million years old.

1173. Earth was created on a Saturday evening, on October 22nd, in the year 4004 B.C.

1174. If the events on Earth from the beginning of time until now were compressed into just 24 hours, the existence of humans would start at 40 seconds before midnight.

1175. The longest flight of a chicken on an airplane was about 13 seconds long.

1176. The first telephone book was made in 1878, and it only contained 50 names.

1177. The creation of instant coffee was only in 1901.

1178. We only started using plastic bottles for soft drinks in 1970. Before, we used glass bottles and metal cans.

1179. The Chinese have been using fingerprints to identify one person from another as far back as 700 A.D.

1180. The Taj Mahal is one of the oldest buildings in the world.

1181. As far as we know, most dinosaurs would have only lived for a little over a hundred years.

1182. Dinosaurs were known to have ruled the earth for over 165 million years.

# Facts About Space Flight

1183. A spacesuit weighs about 280 pounds.

1184. It takes 45 minutes to put on a spacesuit.

1185. The Soviet Union launched the first satellite, Sputnik I, in 1957.

1186. The first US satellite was Explorer 1. It was launched in 1958.

1187. It took 115 minutes for Explorer 1 to orbit the Earth.

1188. The space shuttles were the world's first reusable spacecraft.

1189. Each space shuttle astronaut was allowed 3.8 pounds (1.7 kg) of food per day.

1190. All space food is individually packaged and precooked, except for fresh fruit and vegetables.

1191. The final space shuttle mission was in 2011.

1192. The International Space Station (ISS) launched in 1998. It was a joint venture between the United States and Russia.

1193. Some people believe the 1969 moon landing was fake.

1194. Astronauts have reported the moon smells like wet ashes or gunpowder.

1195. Cartoon dog Snoopy is the safety mascot for NASA.

1196. The ISS is the most expensive object ever created. It cost more than $120 billion to build.

1197. The ISS has been continually occupied by astronauts from different countries since 2000.

1198. Many astronauts get "space sick." Symptoms include nausea, dizziness, headaches, and vomiting.

1199. Many animals have been sent into space, including dogs, monkeys, chimpanzees, mice, and frogs.

1200. The first human to travel to space was Yuri Gagarin from the Soviet Union in 1961.

1201. A 1967 international law prevents any nation from owning planets, stars, or moons.

1202. ISS astronauts get weekends off.

1203. Space is full of junk, including old satellites, rockets, dropped tools, and gloves.

1204. Scientists think there are about 500,000 small pieces of space junk orbiting the Earth.

1205. Space junk that is 500 miles (805 km) above Earth will orbit for decades.

1206. All space junk is the property of the nation that built it.

1207. A spacecraft has to travel 15,000 miles (24,140 km) per hour to break free of Earth's gravity.

1208. It took almost 528,000 gallons (2 million liters) of fuel to launch the space shuttle into space.

1209. In 1959, an unmanned Soviet spacecraft crash-landed on the moon.

1210. Valentina Tereshkova of the Soviet Union was the first woman in space in 1963.

1211. On July 20, 1969, Neil Armstrong and Buzz Aldrin became the first people to walk on the moon.

1212. Armstrong, Aldrin, and Michael Collins traveled 250,000 miles (402,000 km) to the moon and back.

1213. In 2001, a private citizen named Dennis Tito spent $20 million to spend a week on the ISS.

1214. Six Apollo missions landed on the moon between 1969 and 1972. They were Apollo 11, 12, 14, 15, 16, and 17.

1215. Apollo 13 was supposed to land on the moon, but an explosion onboard meant it had to turn back to Earth.

1216. In 2012, NASA sent the Curiosity robot rover to Mars.

1217. Curiosity weighed about a ton and was the size of a car.

1218. Curiosity traveled around the surface of Mars, collected samples, and sent photos back to Earth.

1219. A complete NASA spacesuit costs $12 million.

1220. Most of that cost is for the backpack and control module.

1221. The footprints on the moon will be there for millions of years because there is no wind to blow them away.

1222. Spacecraft travel so fast when they re-enter Earth's atmosphere that the friction creates intense heat.

1223. Spacecraft have special tiles to reflect heat so the ship doesn't burn up on re-entry.

1224. There have been three major disasters in the American space program.

1225. In 1967, three astronauts were killed in a launch pad fire onboard the Apollo 1 space capsule.

1226. In 1986, the space shuttle Challenger exploded after takeoff. All seven astronauts, including school teacher Christa McAuliffe, were killed.

1227. Seven astronauts died aboard space shuttle Columbia in 2003 when it disintegrated upon re-entering Earth's atmosphere.

## High-Flyng Facts About Airplanes

1228. Airplanes can fly because air moves faster over the top of the airplane wing than it does underneath. This creates lift.

1229. The Wright brothers achieved the first airplane flight in 1903.

1230. The first flight lasted just 12 seconds. The plane traveled 120 feet (37 meters). Orville Wright was the pilot.

1231. Orville's brother, Wilbur, later flew 852 feet (260 meters) in 59 seconds on the same day.

1232. In 1927, Charles Lindbergh became the first person to fly solo across the Atlantic Ocean.

1233. The trip took Lindbergh 33½ hours to fly from New York to Paris.

1234. Lindbergh might be the most famous person to cross the Atlantic, but he wasn't the first. John Alcock and Arthur Whitten Brown crossed the Atlantic in 16 hours in 1919.

1235. Alcock and Brown won a large cash prize for their flight.

1236. The Concorde was a supersonic plane that flew between Europe and New York from 1976 to 2003.

1237. The Concorde could fly up to 1,354 miles (2,179 km) per hour.

1238. The Concorde holds the record for fastest transatlantic flight: 2 hours, 52 minutes, and 59 seconds to fly from London to New York.

1239. World War I was the first war to use airplanes in battle.

1240. After the war, many military pilots became barnstormers.

1241. Barnstormers delighted crowds by performing dives and spins in the air.

1242. Barnstorming shows often included performers who walked on the wings of the airplane while in flight.

1243. Early airplanes had open cockpits. Pilots were exposed to rain, wind, ice, and freezing temperatures.

1244. A Boeing 747 jet has 6 million parts.

1245. Each engine on a Boeing 747 weighs almost 9,500 pounds (4,300 kg).

1246. A 747's fuel tank holds almost 48,445 gallons.

1247. The "black boxes" that contain a flight's data are actually orange. The bright color makes them easy to find.

1248. At any moment, 5,000 planes may be flying over the United States.

1249. All pilots who fly internationally must know English. That's so they can communicate safely with air-traffic controllers.

1250. Pilots and copilots eat different meals on a flight. If one of them gets food poisoning, the other one can still fly the plane.

1251. Pilot Chuck Yeager broke the sound barrier in 1947. He was the first person to fly faster than the speed of sound.

1252. The Bede BD-5 microjet is the smallest plane in the world. It weighs only 360 pounds (163 kg) and has a wingspan of 14 ½ feet (4.4 meters).

1253. The longest military plane is the United States' C-5 cargo plane. At almost 223 feet (68 meters) long, it can carry large military equipment, such as tanks and trucks.

1254. The Wright brothers established the world's first test-flight facility near Dayton, Ohio.

1255. That test-flight facility is now called Wright Patterson Air Force Base.

1256. The first woman in the United States who was licensed to fly a plane was Harriet Quimby in 1911.

1257. Quimby became the first woman to fly across the English Channel.

1258. Amelia Earhart was the first woman to fly solo across the Atlantic Ocean.

1259. Airplanes usually fly about 35,000 feet (10,668 meters), or 6.5 miles (11 km), above the Earth.

1260. A commercial jet flies about 550–580 miles (885–933 km) per hour.

1261. The Lockheed SR-71 Blackbird is the fastest plane on Earth. In 1976, this military plane flew 2,193 miles (3,529 km) per hour.

1262. The Blackbird is so fast, it can outfly surface-to-air missiles.

1263. Most planes use autopilot during flight, but pilots control the plane during takeoffs and landings.

1264. In 1985, a plane called Voyager flew around the world without stopping or refueling.

1265. Airbus is working on a transparent plane.

1266. Fear of flying is called aviophobia.

1267. Airplanes that make long flights have secret bedrooms so the crew can nap in flight.

# Out-Of-This-World Facts About Aliens

1268. The study of extraterrestrial life is called astrobiology.

1269. More than 3,000 planets reside outside our solar system. Scientists believe some of them have the conditions to support life.

1270. Life could also exist on planets in other solar systems.

1271. Planets have to be a certain distance from their sun(s) in order for life to survive. Scientists call these areas "the Goldilocks zone" because the temperature is not too hot, not too cold, but just right.

1272. The earliest recorded UFO sighting occurred in 1440 BC. Ancient Egyptian scribes recorded "fiery disks" hovering in the sky.

1273. The ancient Greeks first wrote about extraterrestrial life in 610 BC.

1274. Some people believe the Bible's description of the prophet Ezekiel seeing a "wheel in the sky" was a description of a UFO.

1275. Alien sightings have been reported at many military bases and nuclear power plants.

1276. The first scientific attempt to communicate with aliens was in 1960.

1277. Astronomer Frank Drake tried to contact aliens by using radio signals. He didn't get any answers.

1278. In 1977, Voyager spacecraft included recordings of whale calls, greetings in different languages, and music, in case any aliens found the craft.

1279. The most UFO sightings were recorded between the 1950s and the 1970s.

1280. In 1947, the US Army Air Force reported that it had recovered an alien spaceship in Roswell, New Mexico.

1281. Later, the government said the "spaceship" was actually a top-secret spy device. However, not everyone believes that story.

1282. Nevada's Area 51 is a military site that is closed to the public. Many people believe that alien bodies or spacecraft from Roswell are stored there in secret.

1283. Aliens are often reported to be tall, greenish in color, with very large heads and eyes.

1284. Astronomers Margaret Turnbull and Jill Tartar created a list of more than 17,000 stars that could have orbiting planets that support alien life.

1285. The privately owned SETI Institute in California has been scanning stars for signs of life since 1995. They haven't found anything yet.

1286. SETI stands for The Search for Extraterrestrial Intelligence.

1287. SETI is building a 350-antenna Alien Telescope Array to search for even more aliens.

1288. You can download software from SETI to scan for aliens on your home computer.

1289. Scientists believe that the most likely places for alien life have water sources.

1290. They list four potential alien spots: underground on Mars, Saturn's moon Enceladus, and two of Jupiter's moons, Callisto and Europa.

1291. In 2006, the French Center for National Space Studies broadcast a TV program aimed at extraterrestrials.

1292. Cosmic Connexion was beamed to a star named Errai.

1293. Errai is 45 light-years from Earth. The video won't reach the star until 2051.

1294. In 2007, three US senators created the Advanced Aerospace Threat Identification Program (AATIP). The program is funded by the Department of Defense.

1295. AATIP investigates reports of UFO sightings. Many are from members of the military.

1296. AATIP reports include evidence that UFOs behave in a way that defies the laws of physics.

1297. For example, UFOs travel at extremely high speeds or defy gravity.

1298. AATIP scientists also describe finding objects not made of materials found on Earth.

1299. Beginning in 2007, scientists began recording FRBs, or fast radio bursts. These bursts only last a few milliseconds but give off more energy than our sun does in 24 hours.

1300. Some scientists believe that FRBs, which come from outside the Milky Way, may be signals from an alien civilization on another planet.

1301. A group called METI (Messaging Extraterrestrial Intelligence) was founded in 2015.

1302. In 2017, METI began broadcasting music to a planet about 12 light-years away from Earth.

1303. Barney and Betty Hill claimed that aliens had abducted them in 1961. They described details of the event under hypnosis. But no one knows if their story is true.

1304. In 1977, Ohio's Big Ear Telescope picked up a 72-second burst of sound that came from space. Many scientists think it was a communication from another planet.

1305. The Big Ear transmission is called the Wow Signal because an astronomer was so surprised that he wrote "Wow!" on the printout.

1306. During World War II, many pilots flying over Europe reported very fast, bright lights following their planes.

1307. On March 13, 1997, thousands of people in southern Arizona reported seeing a set of lights moving across the sky in a V formation. The Air Force investigated but no explanation was ever given.

# Chapter 9: Distant matter

# Old Knowledge About Ancient Civilizations

1308. Rome was founded around 753 BC by a king named Romulus. Rome is named after him.

1309. An old story said that Romulus and his twin brother, Remus, were raised by wolves, but that is not true.

1310. Rome had a powerful army.

1311. At one time, the Roman Empire covered all of Europe, plus parts of Africa and Asia.

1312. Ancient Romans ran water to their cities through a series of pipes called aqueducts.

1313. Wealthy Romans used piped water to heat and cool their homes.

1314. Rich Romans ate many exotic foods, including parrots and flamingoes.

1315. Meanwhile, poor Romans ate mostly bread and other grains.

1316. Romans made concrete that is stronger than the concrete we use today.

1317. The first supermarket and shopping mall were found in ancient Rome. The Trajan Market, built around 110 BC, housed more than 150 shops and a large food market.

1318. The ancient Mayans invented a game that was a lot like basketball. However, players could not use their hands or feet to get the ball into the hoop.

1319. The ancient Egyptians invented a form of picture writing

| | called hieroglyphics. |
|---|---|
| 1320. | Egyptian workers often left graffiti carved into the buildings they constructed. |
| 1321. | The Mayans also used hieroglyphics. |
| 1322. | Salt was so valuable in the ancient world that Greeks and Romans used it as money to buy goods and pay wages. |
| 1323. | In 1259 BC, the Egyptians and the Hittites created one of the earliest peace treaties. |
| 1324. | Ancient Egyptians loved to play board games. |
| 1325. | Pharaohs like King Tut even had board games buried with them in their tombs. |
| 1326. | Ancient Egyptians considered animals to be incarnations of gods. |
| 1327. | They kept many pets, including cats, dogs, hawks, lions, and baboons. |
| 1328. | Egyptian pets were often mummified and buried with their owners. |
| 1329. | Ancient Greeks worshipped many different gods. |
| 1330. | Greek myths told fantastic stories about gods and mortals. |
| 1331. | The democratic form of government was invented in ancient Greece. |
| 1332. | No wars or fighting were allowed in the three months before the ancient Greek Olympic Games so that athletes and spectators could travel safely. |
| 1333. | Ancient China was ruled by powerful families called dynasties. |

1334. The dragon is the symbol of Chinese emperors. Some emperors even believed they were descended from dragons.

1335. Ancient Ghana sat on an enormous gold mine. The civilization was so rich that even dog collars were made of gold.

1336. The ancient city-state of Carthage was one of the most powerful empires. It was located in present-day Tunisia.

1337. Carthage craftsmen were extremely skilled at making furniture.

1338. Carthage was destroyed by the Roman empire.

1339. The solar system was first mentioned in an ancient Indian text called the Rigveda.

1340. Chess was invented in ancient India.

1341. So was the game Snakes and Ladders.

1342. Diamonds were first mined in India around 700 BC.

## *About Dinosaurs, Ya Dig?*

1343. Dinosaurs first appeared about 230 million years ago.

1344. They became extinct about 65 million years ago.

1345. Scientists believe a giant meteorite hit the Earth and wiped out the dinosaurs.

1346. The word dinosaur means "fearful lizard" in Greek.

1347. The word was first used in 1842.

1348. Scientists have discovered more than 700 different kinds of dinosaurs.

1349. Meat-eating dinosaurs laid long, thin eggs.

1350. Plant-eating dinosaurs laid eggs that were round.

1351. Big dinosaurs were probably too heavy to sit on their eggs. They might have piled plants on top instead.

1352. Spinosaurus had tall, thin spines on its back. They measured up to 7 feet (2 meters) high.

1353. Scientists think Spinosaurus's spines created a sail that cooled the dinosaur's body.

1354. Some dinosaurs swallowed stones to grind up their food.

1355. When large dinosaur bones were first discovered, people thought they were dragon bones.

1356. Cryolophosaurus was discovered near the South Pole.

1357. It was the first dinosaur discovered in Antarctica.

1358. T. Rex had the largest teeth of any dinosaur. They were the size of bananas.

1359. A T. Rex named Sue is the largest and most complete T. Rex skeleton ever found.

1360. You can visit Sue at Chicago's Field Museum.

1361. T. Rex's brain was twice the size of the brains of other giant meat eaters.

1362. Diplodocus had a 20-foot-long (6-meter-long) tail.

1363. Mamenchisaurus's neck was more than 30 feet (9 meters) long.

1364. That's longer than any animal that ever lived.

1365. T. Rex could eat up to 500 pounds (230 kg) of meat in one bite.

1366. Stegosaurus was 30 feet (9 meters) long but had a tiny brain.

1367. Stegosaurus had a second "brain," or nerve center, at the top of its tail.

1368. Many dinosaurs had hollow leg and arm bones. This helped them run fast.

1369. More dinosaurs have been found in the United States than any other country.

1370. The smallest dinosaur found in North America was just 2 feet (0.6 meter) long. It weighed about 2 pounds (0.9 kg).

1371. Giganotosaurus was a real giant! This dino was 5 feet (1.5 meters) longer and almost 6,000 pounds (2,700 kg) heavier than T. Rex.

1372. Giganotosaurus was discovered in Argentina.

1373. Dinosaur fossils have been found on every continent.

1374. Argentinosaurus is the world's largest dinosaur. It weighed 100 tons.

1375. The world's largest bone belongs to Argentinosaurus. This dino's backbone weighs 2 tons.

1376. Deinocheirus's name means "terrible hand." It had three 10-inch (25-cm) claws on each arm.

1377. Parasaurolophus had a domed head. It could blow air through a tube to create a trumpeting sound.

1378. The smallest adult dinosaur fossil belongs to Lesothosaurus. It was about the size of a chicken.

1379. The Dinosaur Trail is a series of preserved dinosaur footprints in Colorado.

1380. A group of plant-eating dinosaurs called sauropods are the largest land animals that ever lived.

1381. They weighed up to 88 tons.

1382. Sauroposeidon is the tallest known dinosaur. It was about 61 feet (18.5 meters) tall.

1383. Megalosaurus was the first dinosaur to be named, back in 1824. Its name means "great lizard."

1384. The first stegosaurus skeleton was found in Colorado.

1385. Roy Chapman Andrews was the first person to find a dinosaur nest. He found it in the Gobi Desert in 1923.

1386. Some dinosaur eggs were as big as basketballs.

1387. Most meat eaters walked on two feet. They could move faster and use their hands to grab prey.

1388. Plant-eating dinosaurs walked on four feet to support their heavy bodies.

1389. Scientists have found fossilized prints of dinosaur skin.

1390. All dinosaurs laid eggs.

1391. Scientists make mistakes. Gideon Mantell thought iguanodon's big thumb claw was located on top of its nose. It took 40 years to fix that mistake.

1392. Most scientists believe that dinosaurs evolved into birds.

# Chapter 10: The mysteries of the body

## Brain-Busting Brain

1393. The human brain weighs about 3 pounds.

1394. About 60 percent of the brain is made up of fat.

1395. Your brain isn't fully formed until age 25.

1396. Brain development occurs from back to front.

1397. The first successful brain surgeries were performed during the Stone Age.

1398. Some brain surgeries are done with the patient still awake.

1399. The brain has three parts: the medulla, cerebrum, and cerebellum.

1400. The medulla is the lower part of your brain. It controls breathing, swallowing, and other automatic functions.

1401. The cerebellum is above the medulla. It is in charge of sensory functions and movement.

1402. The cerebrum is the largest part of the brain. It interprets speech, reasoning, and emotion.

1403. The cerebrum has two parts, the right hemisphere and the left hemisphere.

1404. Each hemisphere controls the opposite side of the body.

1405. The brain generates about 23 watts of electricity. That's enough to power a light bulb.

1406. There are about 100,000 miles (160,934 km) of blood vessels in the brain.

1407. There are about 100 billion neurons, or nerve cells, in the brain.

1408. Neurons generate electrical impulses that send information from one cell to another.

1409. Information can move at a speedy 268 miles (431 km) per hour along neurons.

1410. Your brain is always active, even when you are sleeping.

1411. The sperm whale has the largest brain of any animal. It weighs up to 20 pounds (9 kg). But that's really small compared to the whale's huge size.

1412. Most of a sperm whale's huge head is filled with fat.

1413. The human brain grows about three times in size during the first year of life.

1414. The brain interprets pain signals from other parts of the body, but the brain itself cannot feel pain.

1415. The brain gets smaller as we get older.

1416. Brains lose some of their ability to think and remember things by the late twenties.

1417. Your brain uses about 20 percent of the oxygen in your body.

1418. If brain cells are deprived of oxygen, they will die.

1419. Synesthesia occurs when a person mixes up sensory signals. People with this condition can hear colors or see sounds.

1420. Telephone numbers in the United States are seven digits long because that's how many numbers our short-term memory can hold on to.

1421. Our brains prefer images over text.

1422. The attention span of the human brain is getting shorter.

1423. The average attention span is now just 8 seconds.

1424. Reading promotes brain development in children.

1425. The human brain is about three times larger than the brains of animals the same size.

1426. Human brains float in cerebrospinal fluid. This fluid cushions and protects the brain from injuries and infections.

1427. Scientists used to think people only used about 10 percent of their brain. Today, we know that we use almost all of the brain.

1428. Your brain is very active while you are dreaming.

1429. A person's brain activity is as unique as their fingerprints.

1430. The brain has more different kinds of cells than any other part of the body.

1431. Dolphin brains are bigger than human brains.

1432. A spider's brain is too big to fit inside its head. It also extends down the creature's legs.

1433. More than half of an octopus's neurons are in its tentacles and suckers. This allows an octopus to solve puzzles with their tentacles.

1434. Leeches have 32 small brains.

1435. A nematode's tiny brain has just 302 neurons.

1436. A woodpecker's skull is made of thick bones with air pockets inside to protect the bird's brain as it bangs against tree trunks.

1437. Crows, ravens, and jays are the smartest birds.

1438. An ostrich's eyeballs are so big that there isn't much room for the bird's brain inside its skull. So this bird's brain is smaller than its eyes.

1439. Whales use half their brain for sleeping and half for breathing. The breathing part of the brain stays awake while the whale sleeps.

1440. A whale keeps one eye open on the side of its brain that is awake while the other eye is closed when it's sleeping.

1441. Dolphins and sea lions do the same thing.

1442. A cockroach can live for a short time without its head or brain.

## Fantastic Things About The Five Senses

1443. Sound waves travel into our ears. These vibrations are picked up by tiny hairs that turn them into electrical signals.

1444. The brain figures out what sounds you are hearing.

1445. If the tiny hairs in your ears are damaged or lost, you will lose your hearing.

1446. Our outer ears are curved to help gather sounds.

1447. Your inner ears are responsible for both hearing and balance.

1448. Your ears keep working even while you are asleep.

1449. The inner ear is found inside the temporal bone, which is the hardest bone in the body.

1450. Some animals do not have outer ears.

1451. Snakes hear through their jawbones.

1452. Fish "hear" by sensing changes in pressure.

1453. There are five different tastes: sweet, sour, salty, bitter, and umami (savory).

1454. Each person has between 2,000 and 10,000 taste buds on their tongue.

1455. Taste buds are also found on the inside of your mouth and throat.

1456. The senses of taste and smell work together. You can't taste something you can't smell.

1457. Taste buds only live for five to ten days.

1458. Your body is constantly producing new taste buds.

1459. Taste buds are the only sensory organs that can regenerate.

1460. Taste buds can protect you from eating spoiled or dangerous foods.

1461. Each taste bud has tiny nerve hairs. These nerves send signals about the taste to the brain.

1462. You don't sense different flavors on different parts of your tongue.

1463. Your eyes can focus on 50 different objects a second.

1464. The brain is the only organ more complicated than the eye.

1465. Your eyes have special cells called rods and cones.

1466. Rods see shapes. Cones detect colors.

1467. The optic nerve has more than a million nerve cells.

1468. Your pupil can contract faster than any other part of your body. It can close in just 1/100th of a second.

1469. Babies can only see black, white, and red until they are about two months old.

1470. Your eyeballs grow as you age.

1471. If your eyeball is too long, you will be nearsighted. If it's too short, you're farsighted.

1472. Parts of your eye can get sunburned.

1473. People can detect at least one trillion scents.

1474. When odors enter the nose, they travel up to receptors at the top of the nose. These receptors send signals to the brain.

1475. Your body produces new scent cells every 30 to 60 days.

1476. Women usually have a better sense of smell than men.

1477. Dogs have about 44 times more scent receptors than humans do.

1478. Each human has their own distinct smell, except identical twins. They smell the same.

1479. The sense of smell has a stronger link to the emotional parts of the brain than any other sense.

1480. Our sense of smell is better later in the day than it is in the morning.

1481. Our sense of smell is stronger in the spring and summer because of added moisture in the air.

1482. About 5 percent of the population is anosmic. They lack the sense of smell.

1483. Touch is the only sense that is found all over the body.

1484. Tiny receptors under our skin send nerve signals to the brain when we touch something.

1485. Some parts of the body have more receptors than others, such as the back.

1486. Your lips, tongue, face, and fingers have the most receptors.

1487. Your back, chest, and thighs have the fewest.

1488. Women usually have a better sense of touch than men.

1489. The skin is the largest organ in the human body.

1490. Scientists think fingerprints amplify the sense of touch.

1491. Scratching an itch feels good because the scratching sends a different signal to our brain that helps it ignore the itch—until you stop scratching, of course!

1492. Touch is the first sense we develop in the womb.

Made in the USA
Monee, IL
12 December 2023